A Lion in the Sun

A Lion in the Sun

*A Background Book on the Rise and Fall
of the British Empire*

BY EDWARD F. DOLAN, JR.

Parents' Magazine Press • New York

Each Background Book is concerned with the broad spectrum of people, places, and events affecting the national and international scene. Written simply and clearly, the books in the series will engage the minds and interests of people living in a world of great change.

Library of Congress Cataloging in Publication Data

Dolan, Edward F   1924-
    A lion in the sun.

    (A Background book)
    SUMMARY: Traces the history of the British Empire
from its birth in the late fifteenth century to its
replacement by the Commonwealth of the present.
    Bibliography: p.
    1. Great Britain—Colonies—History. 2. Common-
wealth of Nations—History. [1. Great Britain—Colonies
—History. 2. Commonwealth of Nations—History]
I. Title.
DA16.D64   325'.342   77-168484
ISBN 0-8193-0533-2
ISBN 0-8193-0534-0 (lib. bdg.)

For Rick and Jean Lyttle

Contents

Introduction

In the years immediately following World War I, the British Empire stood at its zenith. From its headquarters in the collection of tiny, wind-swept Atlantic islands called the United Kingdom, it circled the globe, touching all the world's continents and hundreds of islands in all its oceans. It constituted the greatest, the richest, and the most powerful aggregation of territories ever assembled under one banner, larger by far than the Roman, Spanish, French, and Austrian empires put together.

Emblazoned on that banner was the figure of a golden lion, the symbol of British authority and power. The lion gazed down on Empire holdings that, in all, embraced approximately one-quarter of the earth's surface. They ranged in size from Canada's sprawling 3,895,979 square miles in North America to Pitcairn Island's dot-like two square miles

1

in the Pacific Ocean. They included the country that held the distinction of being, simultaneously, the world's largest island and smallest continent—Australia—and a 175,000-square-mile stretch of totally ice-sheeted and unoccupied territory—the Ross Dependency in Antarctica.

So widespread were the holdings that a popular saying of the day held that "The sun never sets on the British Empire." It was a remark that could be proved by any international time chart. When the hour was midnight in London, the sun was just rising on Ceylon in the Indian Ocean, was overhead at noon in the Pacific's Fiji Islands, and was readying itself to retire for the day in western Canada.

Housed within the Empire at the time were approximately 448 million people of all cultures, colors, languages, and religious beliefs. Representing close to 25 percent of the world's total population, they ranged from Africans, the Maoris of New Zealand, and the Eskimo's of Canada's Northwest Territories to sheepmen in Australia, sugar planters in the West Indies, and rubber planters in Malaysia. Included, on the one hand, were the people of India, whose forefathers were practicing delicate cosmetic surgery before the birth of Christ; and, on the other, the tribesmen of North Borneo, who continued to live in the 1920s as did their ancestors in the Stone Age. Of the total Empire population, only some 55 million persons—or roughly one in every eight—were of British extraction.

The Britisher of the day had only to spin a globe of the world slowly to grasp, almost at a glance, the immensity of his Empire. There, seen immediately and easily, were, first, its major continental holdings.

Looking at the Western Hemisphere, he could see Canada and its Northwest Territories in North America, British Honduras in Central America, and British Guiana in South America. His eye could then move across the Atlantic to Africa, where the Empire's possessions began at the Dark Continent's southern tip and extended northward all the way to Egypt. Farther east, deep into the Indian Ocean, he could sight giant India, sultry Burma, and the Malay Peninsula. Finally, out in the South Pacific, there was Australia. Sprinkled among these major holdings were smaller continental possessions, among them Aden at the mouth of the Red Sea and Gibraltar on the north side of the opening into the Mediterranean Sea.

As his eye traveled over the globe from one continent to another, it would come upon the Empire's major island holdings. There was Newfoundland off the coast of Canada, the islands of the West Indies in the Caribbean Sea, and two-island New Zealand some 1,200 miles to the east of Australia. To the north of Australia, and ranging up through the Pacific, there were the holdings on New Guinea and Borneo, and then such island groups as the Solomons, the Samoans, and the Fijis. In the Indian Ocean there was Ceylon at the foot of India and, over near Africa, the Mauritius and Seychelles clusters. And in the Mediterranean there were Malta and Cyprus, the first considered a part of Europe, the second a part of Asia.

More difficult by far to see on any globe—indeed, some were no more than mere flecks of the cartographer's pen— were the Empire's lesser island holdings. The eye could find them everywhere. They included Ascension, St. Helena, and

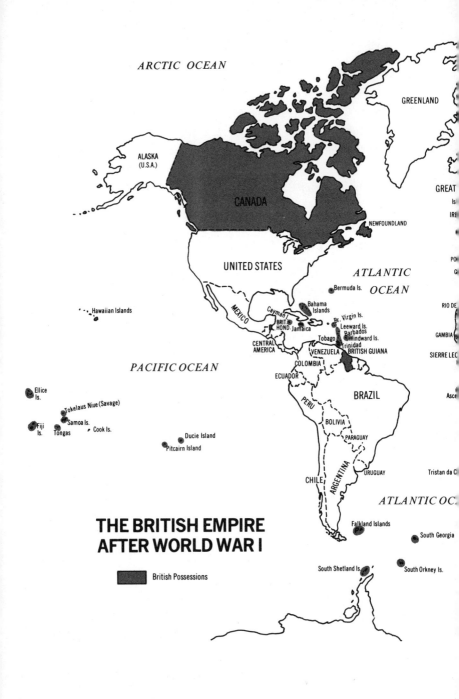

THE BRITISH EMPIRE
AFTER WORLD WAR I

British Possessions

the Falklands in the South Atlantic, the Aucklands, the Cooks, and the Tongas in the South Pacific, and Cocos-Keeling, Heard, and McDonald in the Indian Ocean.

Despite their size, many of these tiny holdings made valuable contributions to the Empire. Some, such as South Georgia deep in the Atlantic, maintained busy and profitable fishing and whaling stations. Others, among them the Tongas, provided the world with such staples as fruits and copra. Many served as fueling stations along the Empire trade routes. Some—the Chathams and Antipodes of New Zealand waters, for example—were held for strategic reasons, principally because of their nearness to larger Empire possessions. Many, on the other hand, were of little or no significance, some being uninhabited chunks of rock sticking up out of the sea.

There could be no doubt, however, about the value of the Empire's major holdings. All were rich in natural resources. In some, they were particularly blessed: they supplied about 1,000 million bushels of the world's annual wheat crop of some 5,000 million bushels; they grew over 250,000 tons of its annual tea crop of approximately 800,000 tons; Australia alone accounted for a major share of the world's wool production, housing about 100 million of the earth's estimated 600 million sheep. In other products, notably coffee, petroleum, and coal, the Empire's possessions were less well endowed.

But, unfailingly, they made good use of their resources, even those with which they were not abundantly graced. They consistently accounted for one-quarter of the world's annual trade, and had done so since the beginning of the twentieth century. They exported to each other and to other countries hundreds of commodities each year, from such basics as foodstuffs and ores to such luxuries as delicate silks and rums.[1]

Now, how was this vast geographic and economic complex managed? How was it governed? What held it together, welding its diverse lands and peoples into a comprehensible whole? Surprisingly, there was no dictatorial ruler, no single secretariat, no single legislative body that controlled the realm. Instead, it consisted of many political entities in many different forms. It is but a slight exaggeration to say that there were almost as many forms of government within the Empire as there were possessions. By the twentieth century the British had become experts at designing form to fit the need, and it was this expertise in political flexibility that made it possible for them to hold intact a goliath of conflicting cultures, languages, and loyalties.

Heading the list of governmental types within the framework of the Empire were the "dominions," such as Australia, Canada, New Zealand, and the Union of South Africa, where the citizens enjoyed complete self-government, maintaining their own parliaments and running their own internal affairs. Next came the "colonies"—which ranged from such continental holdings as British Guiana, British Honduras, and Nigeria to island possessions including Jamaica, Hong Kong, and the Falklands—where the rule extended all the way from locally elected legislative councils to governor-generals appointed by the Crown. Then there were the "protectorates" and "dependencies," administered either by the dominions or the home government at London.

(When they were administered by the home government at London, the dependencies were called "Crown dependencies.") The miniscule islands clustered around New Zealand were examples of dependencies under dominion rule; the Channel Islands and the Isle of Man in the Irish Sea were Crown dependencies; and such African areas as Swaziland and British Somaliland were designated as protectorates. Next were the "protected states." They were ruled by sultans, rajahs, or tribal chiefs with the advice of resident British officials and under a variety of treaties with the Crown. Included among their numbers were Zanzibar, the Maldive Islands, and the Tongas.

There were even "condominiums," ruled jointly with another nation; the Anglo-Egyptian Sudan was a prime example of this category, maintained as it was under a governor-general appointed by Egypt, but serving with British consent. Finally, in the wake of World War I, there were the "mandates," those former enemy possessions such as Palestine on the Mediterranean, Togoland and the Cameroons in Africa which had been awarded to the British by the League of Nations. The next years would see them reassigned as trust territories or dependencies, to be governed by the dominions, the larger and more independent of the colonies, or the Crown itself.

In the 1920s, when the British Empire stood at its zenith, it was little more than three centuries old. Its pliant tapestry of government had taken shape not from one man's inspiration nor from any single creed or doctrine but from the combination of trial, error, stupidity, brilliance, dogged determination, and astonishing foresightedness. On the one hand, there were years marked by ignorance, greed, cruelty, neglect, and blunder. But, on the other, there were the admirable leadership and the technical skill that brought such countries as the restless and always-divided India into greater single units than ever before and readied them—as perhaps they could never have readied themselves—for the twentieth century. And there was the sensitivity to the responsibility owed to those less advanced and less sophisticated—"the white man's burden," as the Britisher of the day would have haughtily put it—a phrase perhaps too superior in tone for modern ears, but one that still makes clear his recognition of his duty to assist and better the lot of his less advantaged fellows. And, finally, in the late nineteenth and early twentieth century, there was the growing awareness of the worldwide trend toward governmental self-determination and the preparation within the framework of the Empire for its eventual flowering.

The purpose of this book is to tell the story of the development of that grand tapestry; to follow the lion—that golden symbol of British power—as he moved through the world until, wherever he looked, the sun was always overhead.

The story of the British Empire began late in the fifteenth century, shortly after history had rung up the curtain on the Age of Discovery. In describing the Empire's eras of growth between those days of wooden sailing ships and the automobile years of the post-World War I period, historians bring two terms into play—the "First Empire" and the "Second Empire."

Beginning with the first westward voyages of John Cabot late in the closing decade of the fifteenth century, the First

Empire continued until the surrender at Yorktown and the loss of the North American colonies. British expansion during the period was centered on a narrow stretch of American seacoast from present-day Maine on the north to the Carolinas and Georgia on the south and on a sprinkling of Puritan-settled islands in the West Indies. It was an expansion motivated almost exclusively by the desire for commercial trade—a trade designed to benefit the merchants at home at the expense of the overseas holdings. The merchants, for example, made certain that the value of raw goods shipped to the mother country never exceeded the value of manufactured goods shipped out. Further, Parliament passed the Navigation Acts, which, with few exceptions, restricted to British ships the movement of colonial cargo, a maneuver that throttled New World trade with other nations and infuriated the colonists. While planters struggled in the tropical West Indies to grow sugar cane, and settlers battled with the North American wilderness to carve out a foothold there, merchants, stock manipulators, and shipowners back home in Britain grew rich. The result: an all-too-easily anticipated flowering of colonial dissent.

Yet, despite such unfair policies, the New World plantations and colonies grew, thanks in the main to religious and economic problems in the mother country. At first, the overseas holdings were ruled by the provisions in their Crown-sanctioned charters, but as the settlements grew, representative government came into being. Colonial self-government might have continued to flourish had not London, nervous over French expansion in the New World and elsewhere, seen it as one more threat to British power. In 1680, to strengthen its control over its holdings, Britain passed charter revisions that placed the West Indies and the North American colonies under the rule of royal governors. Thus, another error in judgment was added to the long list of blunders, misunderstandings, and frictions that ultimately led to the American Revolution and the fall of the First Empire.

Immediately, however, Britain set about building the Second Empire, having already made inroads into Canada and the sprawling complexity that was India. From these two points, so distant from each other, she was to spread her influence throughout the world.

Trade played a vital role in the construction of the Second Empire, as it had in the First. The loss of the American colonies, however, had hurt British pride as well as pocketbooks, and the loss of pride, especially, now prompted serious questioning of past commercial policies. Free trade became accepted as a fairer and far more stable foundation for growth and gradually replaced the many restrictive measures that had seeded the disaster of revolution. Further, during the First Empire, Britain had evolved from a minor agricultural country to an industrial power of consequence, and its merchants and manufacturers were now able to back free trade and endure its competition on an equal footing with other nations. The decision in favor of free trade—and the industrial might to nurture the new policy—put the Second Empire on a firm footing.

But free trade by itself did not deserve all the honors. Other factors of equal importance contributed to the growth of the Second Empire.

There was, to begin with, the eighteenth-century blooming of scientific curiosity which sent British expeditions out to study the marvels and curiosities beyond faraway horizons. In addition to bringing home samples of odd flora and fauna and astonishing all Europe with their notes of strange customs and peoples, they left their nation's flag on the lands they had chanced upon. It was this curiosity that prompted the three Pacific voyages of Captain James Cook and netted Australia and New Zealand for the Empire.

Next, there were the victories that broke the back of the competing French in India and the Americas. And next, the growing awareness (it had begun during the First Empire) that possessions were of a value beyond that of the purely commercial: the holding of distant ground added to the mother country's international prestige and was, in many instances, a vital matter of military security. And, finally, there was the successful conclusion of the Napoleonic Wars, leaving Britain, though exhausted, more powerful than ever and freer than ever for overseas expansion.

As the Second Empire grew, so did the British sense of responsibility to its holdings, a responsibility that shone through the error, the cruelty, and the avarice of individual men. Early in the nineteenth century, when humanitarianism was becoming a political force, Parliament outlawed the slave trade (1807) and soon thereafter banned slavery (1835). Then, with the lessons of the Revolution still stingingly in mind, it encouraged self-rule in the colonies with predominantly white populations. These colonies, which began under all-powerful royal governors, were first given appointed councils. Gradually, more and more council members were allowed to be elected and, inevitably, the responsibilities and independence of the councils were increased.

While it is true that at first a resident had to own property to vote and hold office, the colonies did secure increasing control of local affairs under this pattern. In the end, fully representative government was to emerge.

In the mid-nineteenth century, with Canada, Australia, and New Zealand moving toward complete self-rule, new territories were rapidly added to the Empire. Despite competition from other expansionist nations, Britain acquired possessions throughout Asia, extended her control in India, and then consolidated her South African holdings after a two-and-a-half-year war with the Boers. Further additions came with the dawn of the twentieth century, climaxing with the mandates awarded by the League of Nations at the close of World War I. These latest prizes brought the Empire to the peak of its wealth and power.

They also marked the close of the Second Empire.

Not only did the Second Empire begin to wane, but the concept of empire itself started to die in the 1920s. Its death was made inevitable by changing world politics and attitudes. Even the most flexible of British overseas policies could not stem the tide of nationalism that followed World War I. Nor could they resist the outcries against those instances in which trade and other economic controls had been unfair. Nor the rage and insult of indigenous populations offended by the racial snobbery of many white colonials. As a result, the turbulent social characteristics of modern times were born and they led to the era—it continues to this day—that some historians call the "Third Empire" and that others have christened the "Age of Commonwealth."

What were the changes that occurred within the Empire

and made this new era possible? To name but a few: privileges in Egypt, including reservations on the economically and militarily strategic Suez Canal, had to be surrendered; rights in Iraq were returned to the Arabs; concessions for self-government were made in India and later in parts of Africa; the lastest of uprisings in Ireland, begun in the Easter Week of 1916, saw the southern regions of the country designated as the Irish Free State in 1922.

Britain acknowledged the irresistible wave of change and stabilized her suddenly floundering Empire with the Statute of Westminster. Adopted by Parliament in 1931, it established the British Commonwealth of Nations, the framework within which certain of the Empire's most advanced and independent holdings could join the mother country as equal partners while others less advantaged, remaining within the older framework of Empire, were prepared for some future day of equality. Designated as the first equal partners in the Commonwealth were the United Kingdom itself (England, Wales, Scotland, and Northern Ireland), Canada, Newfoundland, Australia, New Zealand, the Union of South Africa, and the Irish Free State.

The statute formally launched the Third Empire or Commonwealth era.

Since the day of the statute's adoption, the Empire has undergone many changes, not the least of them being the gradual disappearance of the word "Empire" itself in favor of the term "Commonwealth." The changes have been most pronounced since World War II. In the years since Dunkirk, Tobruk, and Normandy, the Union of Burma has departed the Commonwealth to become a republic, as has the Irish Free State, which has been the Republic of Ireland since 1949. Newfoundland has been absorbed as the tenth province in the Canadian federation. Ceylon, India, and the geographically divided Pakistan have all won status as equal partners in the Commonwealth, with the last recently beset by an upheaval which resulted in one of its segments emerging as the independent state of Bangladesh. African nations have been granted sovereignty, some remaining within the Commonwealth, some striking out on their own. And, even as this is being written, Belize (British Honduras) is preparing to shed its colonial robes and step forward as an independent country.

The Commonwealth era marked the end of the Empire as the Britisher of the 1920s and his forefathers knew it. Born in our time has been the collection of states that—loosely organized but tightly bound together, often by the cords of common language, often by similar political institutions and viewpoints, and often by the advantages of mutual commerce and defense—is still recognized across the world as one of the wealthiest and most powerful unions in history.

This sketch of Empire history, from the close of the fifteenth century to the present, is intended to serve as the background against which this book is written. The story of the British lion's advance to and beyond the point where "the sun never set" on his Empire can best be told in three parts—The Dawn (First Empire), Noon (Second Empire), and Sunset (Commonwealth times).

We join him now for his walk in the sun.

It is the hour before the dawn.

Part One
The Lion at Dawn

Chapter One

The Hour Before Dawn

CINNAMON, PEPPER, CLOVES, pain-killing drugs, sweet perfumes, fine silks, intricately woven tapestries, rubies, and pearls—these were the products that gave the world its Age of Discovery and its British Empire.

They were but a handful of the luxuries found in the Far East and, by the time of the First Crusades in the eleventh century, they were available on a very limited scale to Europeans. But, between then and the beginning of the fourteenth century, the men of the austerely endowed West who traveled out to battle the Infidel in the Holy Land came upon them in great number and learned the full enjoyment of their use.

Thanks to word brought home by the Crusaders, a vigorous demand for the products occurred throughout Europe, a demand that was further sharpened when the Italian mer-

chant-adventurer Marco Polo returned to his Venice home in
1295 after two decades in the Orient and wrote a book about
the wondrous sights and fabulous wealth he had seen there.
At first, however, some Europeans thought Marco Polo
guilty of exaggeration and, even when he was on his death-
bed, he was urged to confess his lies and cleanse his soul, a
plea that he weakly but adamantly refused. Soon, however,
the tales of other travelers to the East, though admitting that
he had been prone to exaggeration, largely supported all that
Polo had said.

With the European appetite whetted, the Italian cities of
Genoa and Venice became the centers of the Far Eastern
trade. Goods were shipped overland from the Orient by
camel caravan to Acre on the eastern coast of the Mediterranean and then sailed to Venice and Genoa for distribution
to Europe. The demand was enough to satisfy the most ambitious of merchants, but the trade posed as many headaches
as profits—in fact, far more. First, there were time and distance; months of rough travel, resulting in much breakage
and loss of precious cargo, were required to get the shipments across the necessary several thousand miles. Second,
the costs of transit were so high that, when merchandise
finally reached Italy, it had to be priced beyond the means of
all but the richest if any sort of profit was to be realized.
Finally, and most important, there was the ever-present question of danger. The overland route ran directly through the
lands of the Ottoman Empire, and savage Turkish bandits
roamed the trail, attacking the caravans, making off with the
cargoes, and leaving behind the slaughtered bodies of camels
and traders to rot in the sun.

The expense and the risk were such that the idea of finding safer routes eventually took shape in European minds. Obviously, the safest routes—and the ones promising the swiftest travel—were those that ran through the sea. It was the quest for such passages in the latter half of the fifteenth century that opened the Age of Discovery and netted the world far more than an increase in Oriental commodities. The age revealed an entire, hitherto-unsuspected world to European eyes.

By virtue of her location, Great Britain should have been among the first nations to seek out sea lanes to the riches of the Far East. At her doorstep lay the Atlantic, running west to the as-yet-undiscovered North American continent, southwest past another undetected continent to a storm-tossed juncture with the Pacific, and due south down the African coast to the Indian Ocean. She had only to launch her ships and pick a direction for them to sail, and success would have been hers. She would have come to the spice ports of the Orient or, better yet, to the fabulously wealthy New World that lay between.

But, when the curtain went up on the Age of Discovery, the island nation was not yet ready for the costs and the political risks of exploration, no matter how great the promised rewards. She was as yet a small agricultural country with no great number of naval or commercial ships at her command. Also, she was just out of the Hundred Years War and, without the time even to draw a free breath, already into the Wars of the Roses. Behind her were all the battles that had resulted in the loss of her holdings in France except for the Channel port of Calais. At hand was the thirty-year internal struggle between the Houses of York and Lancaster over the throne of England. It was to be a period of inter-mittent bloodshed that would finally close with Lancaster's Henry Tudor crowned as Henry VII.

Too, Great Britain was still a long way from being the United Kingdom that she would one day become. For cen-turies now, the English kings had attempted to corral Scot-land, Wales, and Ireland under their banner, and the job was perhaps about half done. Since the twelfth-century days of Henry II, inroads had been made deep into Ireland, but no one could say that the spirited island had come anywhere near genuflecting to English authority. Wales had been overrun and annexed by Edward I in the thirteenth century, but the battle to bring Scotland to heel still raged and would continue to do so until Edinburgh Castle fell during the reign of William and Mary in 1691.

And so Britain was too small, too much involved in in-ternal discord, too tired, and her treasury too drained by the war in France for the drama that was about to unfold. The chief players, at least in its opening act, were to be Spain and Portugal, both just now breaking free from centuries of Moorish domination and emerging as the lead-ing sea powers of the day. Both were jealous performers who would tolerate no intrusion. Were Britain to dare step on-stage and declare herself a competitor, they would unhesi-tantly retaliate by hunting down her explorer ships and sending them to the bottom. And she would be helpless to stop the slaughter. She was simply without the wherewithal to fight back, and she knew it.

Between 1460 and 1588, the island nation was to gather the strength necessary for overseas expansion. But, while she grew, she was forced to the role of spectator, watching Spain and Portugal, pursued closely by France and the little Netherlands, reap the major spoils of the day.

She watched Portugal, in a series of exploratory thrusts, inch its way patiently down the African coast until, in 1488, Bartholomew Diaz rounded the Cape of Good Hope and stood into the Indian Ocean. Then came news of the men who sailed in his wake—Vasco Da Gama, Pedro Cabral, Ferdinand Magellan, Diego Sequira, and Francisco Serrano. They pushed up the eastern face of Africa, traveled over to the Persian Gulf, moved on to India, and from there finally ventured out into the Pacific, establishing trading posts and military-commercial settlements all along the way. By 1511, Portugal was well settled in the Indian Ocean, and her annual profits in the spice trade there were immense. Competing with her were France and the Netherlands.

The news from Spain was even more exciting. The Spanish, in 1492, put their money on the Genoese-born cartographer, Christopher Columbus, and sent him across the Atlantic to prove his contention (held in common with most educated men of the period) that the world was not a flat dish but a globe—one that would see a ship sailing west from Europe eventually come to anchor in some Far Eastern port. That voyage and the additional three that Columbus made in the next ten years changed the history of the world.

Back to London came the news that, on all four journeys, he had sighted strange lands—from the present-day islands of San Salvador, Cuba, Haiti, and Jamaica to the Central American coast at Honduras. And back came the news that he himself thought them to be a sort of out-sized barrier reef at the fringes of the Orient. And, finally, the news that subsequent explorations were proving him wrong—proving that his lands were actually a part of a vast and rich territory, hitherto hidden from Europe by the Atlantic, that was rapidly showing itself to consist of two continents connected by a thick rope of mountains, jungles, and deserts at their far western extremities. Beyond them, so Vasco Nunez de Balboa reported from the Isthmus of Panama in 1513, lay an ocean as great as the Atlantic, separating them from the Orient by untold miles.

Britain, along with the rest of Europe, added a series of new names to the geographical vocabulary of the day—North America, South America, Central America, the Caribbean Sea, the Gulf of Mexico, and the all-embracing and stimulating "New World." Intently, she watched the Spanish begin to withdraw gold and silver from this New World. So bountiful was the crop that they set aside their quest for the Orient in its favor. And so bountiful was it that Britain felt her first interest in western exploration come to bud. If possible, she, too, wanted some share of the treasure, no matter how small.

That tiny bud of interest is seen in the orders that Henry VII, shortly after his ascension to the throne at the close of the Wars of the Roses, issued to the Italian-born navigator, John Cabot, who was then sailing in the English employ. He directed Cabot to travel west and "discover and find . . . Countries and Regions . . . before this time unknown to all Christians . . ." [2]

The result: in 1497 and again in 1498, Cabot sailed across the Atlantic on a course far north of that traced by Columbus. He touched at Cape Breton Island and Newfoundland, sighted the Grand Banks fishing grounds, and then ventured

as far south as the present-day Carolinas. The voyages gained
two advantages for Britain. First, they established a claim
to the middle and upper regions of North America that was
to come in handy when colonization finally began in earnest.
Second, the sighting of the Grand Banks threw open the
door to a new commercial venture for the little island nation.

Of the two, Britain regarded the latter as the more important. Cabot had traveled to the north to keep well away
from the Spanish and, with the exception of the Carolinas
(which were too close to the Spanish domain for comfort),
the coasts that he had sighted looked barren and bleak,
promising little hope of treasure. But a new and fertile fishing area that, even under the canvas sail of the day, was no
more than two weeks away, with a good wind from astern,
was a different matter. Britain was burdened with a mounting population and her national larder needed constant re-
plenishing. She immediately dispatched several ships westward to work the Banks.

Those first few pioneers eventually grew into a fleet of
some four hundred vessels that regularly sailed from her
ports every summer. Joining Britain at the Banks, once they
heard of the magnificent catches available there, were France,
Spain, and Portugal, all fishing peacefully together, international rivalries forgotten in the business at hand. So plentiful were the fish that any ship could fill its holds to the
hatches, salt its catch ashore at Newfoundland or Nova
Scotia, and raise sail for home in only a few days.

Though it may seem to be nothing more than an interesting historical sidelight, the early fishing at the Banks actually made an important contribution to later British overseas expansion. Prior to the Age of Discovery, Britain had

little tradition of the sea. Her interests had been principally limited to the Channel, which she saw as a water highway to her French possessions. With the Banks fishing industry, she turned many of her coves and inlets into seaports and became intimately acquainted with sailing the Atlantic. She was on her way to becoming the maritime nation that could send settlers, armies, and trade goods to all parts of the world with ease.

Following the Cabot voyages, Britain refrained from further New World ventures throughout the sixteenth century. But not so two of her most daring subjects, the half brothers Sir Humphrey Gilbert and Sir Walter Raleigh. Both felt that a man might well become rich if he could establish a settlement somewhere on the North American coast and not only mine it for gold but farm it for produce that could be traded with the mother country. Both, with the aid of friends, financed expeditions in the late 1500s for the purposes of colonization.

Gilbert was the first to sail, his intention being not only to found a settlement but to establish it as a base for future exploration of a far northern route to the Orient, one safely distant from the Spanish seaways. In 1578, he landed at Newfoundland. The venture failed almost immediately because the people were insufficiently provisioned and unfamiliar with the art of surviving in the wilderness. Gilbert attempted to put down a second colony nearby in 1583, but lost his life when his ship sank in an Atlantic storm.

Raleigh chose a warmer climate—Roanoke Island off the North Carolina coast. Armed with a royal charter, he sent out an expedition to explore the area in 1584 and dispatched his first colonists a year later. The Roanoke settlement also failed. In fact, it simply vanished from sight, as if the wilderness that it had dared to brave had swallowed it whole.

The precise reasons for its disappearance are unknown, but the suggested possibilities are several. Among the villains may have been disease, Indian attack, and—as with the Gilbert enterprise—the lack of basic pioneer skills.

Though unsuccessful, the two settlements established a pattern, similar to that of the French and the Dutch, that was to be followed in much future British colonial development. By using their own funds and those of a few friends, Gilbert and Raleigh initiated the British habit of financing colonization through private companies. Whereas Spain's overseas expansion was in the main accomplished with Crown money, Britain's was the work of private companies blessed with a charter from the government. The habit of private financing began because of a modest national treasury and was continued in wealthier times because of a basic faith in and liking for the free enterprise system.

The two settlements likewise taught Britain a hard lesson. Both drove home the fact that colonization could not be funded by just a handful of people. If settlements were to be successful, if they were to ride out the hardships of their first years and become paying propositions, they had to be backed by a staggering amount of money. This understanding led to the development of what the people of the day called "joint stock" companies, as indeed the Hudson's Bay, East India, and lesser operations were. They were enterprises that could raise the necessary mountains of cash through the small investments of thousands of ordinary citizens—the great-grandfathers of the modern corporation. They were, incidentally, also known as "adventure" companies, with their investors said to be "adventuring" (today, we would say "speculating") their money for possible overseas profits.

Finally, in the idea that led to the founding of the two unsuccessful settlements, we see the first glimmerings of an attitude that was to play a key role in all future empire building. Gilbert and Raleigh recognized a value not only in searching the New World for gold but in tilling its soil for crops. Their insight marked the birth of the understanding that gold and silver were not the only riches available overseas. There was equal wealth to be had from the products of farming, grazing, fishing, logging, manufacturing, and mining. It was an understanding that was to bud steadily over the years and come to full flower with the Industrial Revolution.

But, in the late 1500s, Gilbert and Raleigh were men ahead of their times. Most Britishers, the recently crowned Elizabeth I among them, were principally interested in the New World's gold bullion. Hungrily, they watched it being shipped back to Spain in the holds of an unending procession of high-pooped and fat-hulled galleons. The bullion proved too much of a temptation for some of the nation's more daring seafarers. Financed by private businessmen and quietly sanctioned by the Crown, they swarmed out in small, heavily armed, and highly maneuverable warships to hunt the transports down and divest them of their cargoes. It was a job that they were soon doing with remarkable skill, as witness the success of the best known of their number, Sir Francis Drake. After roaming the Atlantic and Pacific from 1577 to 1580, he returned with his *Golden Hinde* so laden with gold that each of his backers earned 4,600 percent on the investment.

Though there is no word other than "piracy" to describe the activities of Drake and his kind, Britain cheered their forays. Growing steadily stronger as a nation, she was no longer so fearful of Spanish rage. Too, Queen Elizabeth was a Protestant and her hatred of Catholic Spain was well known. She was willing to risk war just to enjoy the spectacle of denuded and embarrassed Spanish ships.

And war she finally got. It came in the mid-1580s and, as matters turned out, it proved to be one of the most fortuitous and consequential struggles in Britain's history. It was the key that opened the door to the nation's overseas expansion, which finally ended three centuries later with a world-girdling empire.

King Philip of Spain pursued the war by assembling a fleet of 130 warships and sending them, manned with pike- and musket-armed infantry, toward England in 1588 for the purpose of invading the upstart island and bringing it to its knees. The fleet was called "The Invincible Armada," but England awaited its arrival calmly, certain that its ships were far too clumsy for effective sea fighting.

Such was the calm, in fact, that Sir Francis Drake, who was playing bowls at the time the Armada arrived off the Plymouth coast and who, as a vice admiral, was destined for a leading role in the coming battle, remarked to his companions, "We have time to finish the game and beat the Spaniards too."

The next days justified his arrogance. A flotilla of agile and heavily gunned British ships sailed out and, according to historians Robert B. Eckles and Richard W. Hale, blasted the attackers with a low, accurate fire at ranges the Spanish could not use. The Armada fled to Calais, but the English admiral, Lord Howard of Effingham, ordered in fireships which sent the Spanish running back into the North Sea. The British pursued and attacked off Gravelines. By that time, both the British and the Spanish were out of gunpowder, for neither had expected such a prolonged and sea-sweeping battle. But now the weather put a stop to the fighting. A fierce storm drove the Spanish far north. The remnants of the Armada rounded Scotland and headed south for home, bringing Philip the news that England would never be conquered. As for the British, they began to boast that "God's winds arose, and his enemies were scattered." [3]

With the victory, Britain's national spirit soared to heights never before attained. In the defeat of the Armada, her people saw, quite correctly, the beginning decline of Spain's power in the world and the beginning ascent of their own. No longer need their island be the small agricultural country it once was. They were ready for new adventures, new conquests, ready to step out and take advantage of the new and rich lands that had been so recently found—and of those that future days would assuredly unveil. And they knew that they now had the strength necessary for the undertaking, for, in sending the Armada fleeing for its life, they had taken command of the North Atlantic. Now, without undue Spanish interference, their ships could sail to North America, plant colonies there, protect them, and, after the first crops were planted and the first cattle put out to pasture, trade with them.

With the disappearance of the broken Armada over the horizon, the sun began to rise.

The morn of Empire was at hand.

Chapter Two

To the New World

BUT MAKE NO mistake.

Do not think that British ships sailed out to found New World colonies and trading posts at the dawn of the seventeenth century only because their nation had defeated the Armada. The victory was a prime mover, yes, but there were several other factors that had long been at work in Britain. All of them had been steadily pushing her toward the day of overseas expansion. The Armada welded them together and, in addition to the strength that it bestowed on the little nation, gave them their final impetus.

Historian Thomas A. Bailey pointed them out. He wrote that economic motivations were strong, that a vigorous middle class had risen, which was providing the country with an active group of merchants who could supply the business leadership and wealth for colonial ventures. He said further

31

that England was burdened with what she thought to be a surplus population, although her four million inhabitants totaled only about half those living in London in the middle of the twentieth century. Further, the woolen industry was spreading, with many farms being turned into grazing lands and with the sheep putting many a farm laborer out of work. The Catholic monasteries and nunneries, which had long cared for the poor, had been seized by the anti-papal Crown, leaving the poor with nothing to do but wander the countryside. In the late 1500s, Bailey writes, the land swarmed with beggars and paupers.

Bailey also notes that English colonization was greatly influenced by the Protestant Reformation. Henry VIII had broken with Rome and had established his own Church of England, installing himself as its head. Many Protestants, particularly those who felt that the new church still contained too many Catholic ideas, thought America a more suitable home for people of their belief. On the other hand, many Catholics, persecuted by the Crown and believing that the king had gone too far in his break with Rome, began to look on the New World as a possible haven.[4]

Historian Merle Burke notes still another factor. He writes that England was evolving from an agricultural to a handicraft nation. As she produced more and more goods, overseas colonies became desirable for two reasons: they would be sources of raw materials needed for the homeland's growing industries; and they would be markets for finished products that could not be absorbed in England itself.[5]

We shall see each of these factors come to the forefront as Britain moved westward and secured her first footholds in the New World. The British advance across the sea was a two-pronged attack, with each prong quite distinct in character from the other.

One prong took explorers and trappers to the Hudson Bay area of Canada, a to-be nation that was then called New France because of the deep penetrations made along the St. Lawrence River and elsewhere by the French. British presence in Canada was prompted strictly by the commerce of trapping and the business of opening up new frontiers. Colonization played little or no part in these first ventures, but was reserved for a later date.

The second prong touched along more than a thousand miles of what was to become the eastern seaboard of the United States and eventually spread as far south as the West Indies and as far east as the Bermudas. Here, British presence was likewise prompted by commerce—not to mention religious influences—but, unlike the Canadian adventure, it was carried out not by trappers and explorers (though they played their parts) but by settlers who built towns, cleared the land, tilled the soil, developed seaports, and established manufacturing centers.

Because of their distinctness one from the other, the stories of the Canadian and American ventures must be told separately. We begin with the American story.

Starting in 1607, the British settled or claimed from other nations sixteen areas along the Atlantic seaboard from Maine on the north to the Carolinas and Georgia on the south. In addition to the Hudson Bay region, it was the only New World territory safely available to the British in the dawning seventeenth century.

Immediately to the south lay Florida with its happier climate, but it was owned by the Spanish; despite the Armada, British interests had no desire to buy extra trouble by intruding on the Spanish possession. Directly north were the St. Lawrence and the beaver- and timber-rich New France. Its population was sparse, consisting principally of fur trappers, for the French were not the most adept of colonizers. But the French guarded their fertile regions jealously, and there was no percentage in inviting trouble there either.

And so there was no choice but to settle between the holdings of these two powers. Britain did so by first sending colonists to the northern end and southern reaches of the Middle Atlantic seaboard and then devoting a century to filling in all the thousands of square miles between.

The sixteen areas in question eventually became the thirteen colonies of Revolutionary War days, with three of the original settlements by then having joined larger colonies. Uniting with their larger neighbors were New Haven, Maine, and Plymouth. The first merged with Connecticut in 1662. The second was purchased by Massachusetts in 1677, while the third merged with Massachusetts in 1691.

In chronological order, the settlements were:

Virginia, 1607; Plymouth, 1620; Maine, 1623; New Hampshire, 1623; Massachusetts, c.1628; Maryland, 1634; Connecticut, 1635; Rhode Island, 1636; New Haven, 1638; North Carolina, 1653; New York, 1664 (originally settled by Dutch colonists, c.1613); New Jersey, 1664; Delaware, 1664 (originally settled by Swedish colonists, 1638); South Carolina, 1670; Pennsylvania, 1681; and Georgia, 1733.

The seed out of which these colonies were to grow was planted in 1606 with the formation of two joint stock com-

panies—the Plymouth Company and the Virginia Company
of London. Both were given charters for New World exploitation by James I, who was then in the third year of his reign
following the death of Elizabeth. The charters granted settlement, development, and trading rights to each company
within given geographical confines. To the Plymouth Company went the northern regions—the area between 41° and
45° north latitude. To the Virginia Company went the southern coast—between 34° and 38° north latitude. The land
between was left open for use by either company.

The seed that was the Plymouth Company failed to ger-
minate. The company landed a contingent of settlers on the
Maine coast at the Kennebec River in 1607, only to have them
find the rigors of the wilderness too taxing. They abandoned
their cabins in the next year and fled home. Maine was destined to await the arrival of the Puritans before seeing a
white colonist again.

It was the seed put down by the Virginia Company that
managed to survive. Planted in May of 1607 alongside the
James River at a point close to Chesapeake Bay, it eventually
came to full leaf as the Jamestown settlement—the first permanent British outpost in the New World.

But it did not grow without terrible hardship. The surrounding river marshes swarmed with mosquitoes, and soon
malaria was rampant among the 104 original colonists. Next,
the James River Indians proved hostile; they ambushed the
newcomers wherever they found them and attacked the settlement on several occasions. Finally, and most dangerous of
all to its welfare, many of the settlers were not eager for the
back-breaking work of pioneering: the clearing of woods,

the fishing, the hunting, the building of cabins, and the planting of crops. Their chief interest lay in the discovery of gold, which would send them back to England rich men, there to live the rest of their lives in luxury. Thanks to their greed, famine stalked Jamestown repeatedly during its first years.

That the settlement managed to survive was due in the main to the efforts of two men: John Smith and James Rolfe, the former an army captain, the latter a farmer.

Smith, who is remembered chiefly in history for his tale of how he was saved from Indian execution by the Indian princess Pocahontas, took command of Jamestown and drove the gold-seekers to the practical tasks of farming with his steely-voiced edict that "He who will not work shall not eat." Then, in 1612, Rolfe discovered that tobacco—the yellow leaf plant that Columbus had first seen smoked by Cuban natives—could be just as easily cultivated at Jamestown as in the Caribbean. There was a ready market for the stuff back home, and the colonists immediately established it as their central crop.

With tobacco, Jamestown won its first measure of security and took the initial step toward the day when the Virginia colony (and then the state of Virginia) would be one of the chief tobacco-growing areas of the Western Hemisphere.

Though economic goals prompted the settlement of Jamestown and eventually put it on its feet, they had little to do with the founding of the second permanent North American colony. Tiny Plymouth was the fruit of religious dispute in England.

Its beginnings as a colony can be traced all the way back

to Henry VIII's break with the Catholic Church. In the years that followed—throughout the reigns of Edward VI, Mary Tudor, and Elizabeth I—the nation was torn by religious strife, with its Catholic and Protestant citizens at constant war with each other. Even within the ranks of the Protestants there was dissension. It was most evident in two groups: the Puritans and the Separatists.

The Puritans acquired their name because they believed Henry's Church of England still retained too many Catholic practices and ceremonies. They wanted to see it rid itself—in their words, purify itself—of these remaining links with Rome. The Separatists agreed, but were convinced there was little or no chance of the goal ever being reached. And so their aim was to leave the Church of England, to separate themselves from it and its too-papal practices.

The stands of the two groups so infuriated the Crown that the Separatists had to flee from England and settle in various parts of the continent. One group made its way to the Dutch town of Leyden, arriving there in 1609 and remaining for a decade. At the end of that time, they knew that they must move on for their children were becoming so imbued with Dutch customs that they were in danger of forgetting their own heritage. But a return to England was out of the question. Only persecution awaited them there. They turned toward the New World.

The group applied to the Virginia Company for permission to cross the Atlantic as colonists. The company agreed, financed them in the sum of seven thousand pounds, and sent them on their way in September of 1620, aboard the ship *Mayflower*. In the bargain struck between the colonists

—now called the Pilgrims—and the company, it was agreed that all earnings realized by the new settlement would be pooled for seven years and then be divided among the shareholders. The Pilgrims were included among the shareholders, each being granted a ten-pound share.

The *Mayflower*'s destination was the coast of Virginia, but it missed its target by a wide mark and arrived off Cape Cod in November. The colonists, after vainly trying to sail south through foul weather, decided to settle where they were. They went ashore at a small bay on December 11, 1620, naming the bay Plymouth Bay and their settlement Plymouth.

Before leaving the ship, 41 of the 102 Pilgrims—all adult males, including 11 servants and 2 seamen—drew up and signed the document known as the Mayflower Compact. Behind its writing was the fact that the vessel had not put in at Virginia Company territory and that, consequently, the terms of the Pilgrims' agreement with the firm no longer applied. The settlers needed some sort of document on which to found and then operate their undertaking. The Compact filled the bill.

It was not, as many people mistakenly think, a precise constitution for Plymouth. Rather, just two hundred words long, it established a general formula for the operation of the colony, stating that Plymouth would maintain a democratic form of government, that its members would bend to the will of the majority, and that it would recognize the overall authority of the Crown. Brief though it was and broad though its principles were, the Compact served as the foundation for Plymouth's political life until the little settlement became a part of the Massachusetts Bay Colony in

1691. Of vital significance to the future was the fact that it provided the first glimmer of the democratic tradition that would one day dominate the American scene and bring the First Empire to a close. It is no exaggeration to say that the Compact was the diminutive forefather of such bodies as Virginia's House of Burgesses and the Continental Congress, and of such documents as the Declaration of Independence and the United States Constitution.

The winter of 1620–21, bitter cold and wind-driven, was a nightmare for the Pilgrims, housed as they were in temporary, makeshift dwellings. Sickness and death immediately took their toll, and the settlers saw their ranks depleted by approximately half. But they were a hardy lot, and when the *Mayflower* raised anchor for home the following spring, not one of the colonists was aboard. They set about building permanent cabins and, assisted by hospitable Indian neighbors, put in their first crops.

From this start, Plymouth grew and prospered. Newcomers joined the settlement and, within a decade, it was a snug, fortified town of some three hundred souls.

Historians point out that, so far as population and economics are concerned, Plymouth never constituted a major New World holding. Its true importance is seen in the fact that it served as the gateway for further British development of the northern seaboard into the giant Massachusetts Bay Colony. In other words, the Pilgrims showed what could be done with the uninviting northern frontier. Other Englishmen in religious difficulty—namely, the Puritans—saw the accomplishments and concluded that they, too, could carve out successful lives for themselves there.

By the late 1620s, life in England was intolerable for the

Puritans. In a continuing effort to bring them to heel, the state hounded and persecuted them without respite. So impossible did the situation become that, taking inspiration from the Separatists, the Puritans elected to abandon the homeland.

With the decision made, a large Puritan group organized a trading company in 1629, christened it the Massachusetts Bay Company, and won for it a Crown charter to establish settlements and trading posts in the Massachusetts area, where, just the year before, a small band of Puritans had built the modest town of Salem. The ordinarily antagonistic Crown, happy to be rid of the troublemakers and pleased at the prospect of further New World development, serenely watched several hundred colonists board eleven ships in 1630 and disappear over the western horizon, hearing later that they had founded two settlements, the first called Charlestown, the second Boston. In time, the latter became the hub of the entire Massachusetts Bay Colony.

Boston was the largest settlement to date to be planted by British hands in the New World. After an initial winter of hardship, it flourished, for the Puritans proved to be men of practical as well as religious bent. Busily, they turned such activities as farming, hunting, fishing, and shipbuilding into major New World industries.

Helping the growth of the Massachusetts colony were the enduring difficult conditions in England. Added now to the burden of religious persecution was a period of economic depression. Unemployment was rife, and the bad times resulted in what is called the "Great Puritan Migration." Lasting from about 1629 to 1640, it saw some seventy-five thousand Puritans depart Britain and take up homes in the West. Approximately one-third of their number arrived at Boston. The remainder headed south to the West Indies, where Spanish strength was much on the decline. They settled on such islands as Barbados, there to build up a commerce in sugar.

Some also made their home on the Bermudas, the collection of western Atlantic islands that had first been visited by Spain's Juan de Bermudez in 1515 and then had been settled by sixty Virginia Company colonists in 1612. The Virginia Company eventually sold its interest in the islands to the Bermuda Company, with the Crown finally taking them under its control in 1684. The Bermudas have remained a British possession to this day.

With the southern settlement of Jamestown and the northern Massachusetts Bay Colony, Britain made secure her foothold on the Middle Atlantic seaboard. Now to come were all the settlements to be founded between the southern and northern points. Many of them took shape because the Puritans, who had come west to escape religious intolerance, turned out to be a pretty intolerant crew themselves.

Their view of religion was bleak and intimidating, and their approach to life was stern and authoritarian. Though they had come to the New World to worship as they pleased, they showed little patience for those in their midst who dared dispute their concepts and values. The result: many colonists with a bent for individualism left Massachusetts to establish settlements of their own.

Among them was Roger Williams, a minister whose preaching in Salem and Plymouth against Puritan attitudes had gotten him into trouble with the authorities. He fled south with a band of followers in 1636 and founded Rhode Island Colony. In the same decade, other colonists similarly out of step with Puritanism moved off—or were banished—to New Hampshire and Maine.

Still others made their way to Connecticut country, founding the Hartford and New Haven settlements. They did so only in part to escape the tyrannies of Puritan rule. They were equally interested in forestalling the Dutch colonization that had begun along the Hudson River with the 1613 founding of the little town of New Amsterdam on Manhattan Island. The Dutch had turned the surrounding region into the colonial holding of New Netherland, and the British were eager to see them go no farther.

The Connecticut settlements effectively cut off the New Netherland expansion in one direction, and then a British naval expedition in 1664 pretty much put an end to Dutch ambitions in North America by sailing up to New Amsterdam and taking the city without firing a single shot. Soon thereafter, the British took control of all New Netherland, including the settlements in New Jersey. They had been built originally by Swedish settlers, but had belonged to the Dutch since 1655. New Amsterdam was rechristened New York, was recaptured by the Dutch in 1673, but was returned to British hands a year later—this time for good.

Newcomers to America accounted for many of the sprouting colonies. Fresh arrivals from Britain put down their roots in South Carolina, while Jamestown pioneers were venturing out to North Carolina. Catholics fleeing persecution in the motherland founded Maryland, their first settlements there being St. Mary's and Baltimore. Quakers, likewise escaping persecution, colonized Pennsylvania, first at Newcastle and then at Philadelphia. Georgia came into being as a haven not only for persecuted European Protestants but for the inmates of Britain's debtors' prisons.

By 1733, all of Britain's Middle Atlantic colonies had been planted. The First Empire was little more than 125 years old. And it was a mere 48 years away from its death at Yorktown. Already on the horizon was the discontent that would culminate in the Revolutionary War.

But, to the north, the fourth in a series of wars between the British and French factions in Canada was about to erupt. While the Revolution would see Britain divested of her Middle Atlantic colonies, the Canadian struggle would leave her in control of that gargantuan northern land, well on the way to establishing her Second Empire.

It is to Canada that we now turn, and the events leading to that triumph.

French interest in Canada began in 1534, when a forty-three-year-old Norman seafarer named Jacques Cartier set out for the New World with two ships and sixty-one men. His purpose was not to found a colony but to locate a waterway through its northern reaches to the spice ports of the Orient —a presumed waterway that, in Europe, was already popularly called the Northwest Passage. With Spain in control of the Caribbean and the southern Atlantic, and with Portugal riding herd on the Indian Ocean, both ready to attack any intruder, the weaker nations of Europe—France, Britain, and the Netherlands—saw the discovery of a northern route as their only way of getting a share of the Far Eastern trade.

They were also searching for a sister route—the Northeast Passage—through the icy waters above the Scandinavian countries and Russia.

In the first of two voyages made between 1534 and 1536, Cartier touched at Newfoundland, charted its west coast down through the Gulf of St. Lawrence, and landed at Prince Edward and Magdalen islands and Cape Gaspé on the New Brunswick coast before returning home. The next year saw him sail across the gulf to the mouth of the St. Lawrence River, there meeting Indians who told him that he had come to the land of "Canada," the Iroquois-Huron word for "village." Using an Indian canoe, he traveled inland along the St. Lawrence, passed the promontory on which present-day Quebec is built, and came at last to the Indian village on which the future city of Montreal would rise. Cartier's journey located no water route to the Orient, but firmly established the first French claim to Canada.

France, however, did not immediately capitalize on the claim. She was, in the mid-sixteenth century, the helpless victim of the same problems that were then besetting Britain —foreign wars and domestic strife, the latter caused by the running dispute between the Catholic and Protestant Huguenot factions in her population. She did not get the better of these problems until the dawn of the seventeenth century, at which time, emerging as a powerful and feared nation, she was at last able to concentrate on Canada. And concentrate she did, with such men as Samuel de Champlain, who established her first permanent New World settlement at Quebec in 1608; Father Jacques Marquette and fur trapper Louis Joliet, who, in addition to the former's missionary work among the Indians, traced the Mississippi River down to its juncture with the Arkansas River, and René La Salle, who ventured even farther south, coming at last to the Gulf of Mexico and claiming all the lands within view for Louis XIV. By the final two decades of the century, French claims in the New World stretched inland through the St. Lawrence basin to the Great Lakes and southward down to the Mississippi for the full width of the future United States. The latter claim joined the Allegheny mountain chain in forming a barrier that prevented British expansion westward from the Middle Atlantic coastline.

The French called their Canadian holding New France. They were not, however, accomplished colonists, and only a few families came west—so few, in fact, that even by 1750 there were only about sixty thousand whites living among the Indians. The cold climate held little appeal for the average Frenchman, accustomed as he was to sunny skies at home. Nor did the harsh and dictatorial rule of the Crown, which had taken over the administration of New France after the failure of the several private companies originally charged with its development. It granted the colonists no degree of self-government and even denied them the right of trial by jury. The final authority in any case was the judge himself.

And so New France was populated mostly by free-booting adventurers who cared little about the whims of an autocratic government. They trapped the beaver- and bear-rich country for furs, explored new lands, stayed out of official sight for months on end, and married into Indian tribes. The country grew up with a liberal sprinkling of trading posts and military forts, but with a handful of stable colonial settlements.

Now, what of Britain's interest in Canada?

She, too, had joined in the sixteenth-century search for a northern passage to the Orient, with her earliest venture in that direction dating back to 1527 when Henry VII sent out two ships under the impossible orders to attempt a Far Eastern landfall by sailing via the North Pole; they never returned and are thought to have been lost somewhere between Greenland and Newfoundland. Next, in 1576, 1577, and 1578, Martin Frobisher was dispatched westward. He reached Baffin Island, but got no farther because his attention was diverted by an ore that he mistook for gold. The ill-fated Sir Humphrey Gilbert now took his turn. A chief purpose of his Newfoundland settlement of 1578, in addition to that of colonization, was to serve as base for future Northwest Passage exploration.

The second decade of the seventeenth century brought Henry Hudson to the forefront. Earlier, this English-born navigator had sailed for the Dutch and had established their claim to the lands along the Hudson River and around the future New York City, but now, in 1610, aboard the fifty-five-ton *Discovery* and under the British banner, he followed the paths of Frobisher and Gilbert. He was to have no better luck than they in locating the Northwest Passage, but, managing to press beyond the southern coast of Baffin Island, he entered the giant bay that now bears his name. He explored its eastern shores and then wintered in James Bay at its southern extremity. He planned further exploration in the spring, but his crew mutinied, mostly out of fear of never seeing home again. Hudson was set adrift in a small boat with his son and several loyal followers. There is no record of their fate. *Discovery* returned to England.

The Hudson, Frobisher, and Gilbert expeditions—and the earlier Cabot visits to the Newfoundland area—all established a British claim to the Canadian regions north of the St. Lawrence basin.

Britain pursued the claim with seventeenth- and eighteenth-century explorations and with the chartering of the Hudson's Bay Company. Chief among the explorations were those of Luke Foxe, who investigated the waterways southwest of Baffin Island in 1631; Samuel Hearne, who hiked and canoed deep inland to the Coppermine River in 1770 and became the first white man to visit the Canadian Arctic Ocean; and Alexander Mackenzie, who in 1789 began a journey that took him all the way to the Pacific Ocean and won him the distinction of being the first white man to make a transcontinental crossing of Canada. The trip required four years to complete.

The Hudson's Bay Company was formed in 1670. According to its charter, which was granted by Charles II, its purpose was twofold. It was to import into Britain the animal furs and skins it obtained, either by hunting or Indian barter, from the lands and waters around the ocean-sized bay, and it was to press for the "discovery of a new passage" to the Orient. It put down its first settlements at James Bay and along the nearby Churchill and Hayes rivers. It restricted its activities to these areas in its opening years, but, when its country finally secured control of all Canada, it spread its outposts as far as the Pacific.

Until 1689, the French and British occupied Canada in

relative peace. The reason was quite simple. Their territories were separated by hundreds of miles of trackless forests and tundra lands. There was no necessity for conflict, for the trappers, explorers, and soldiers of either nation rarely ran into each other and, if they did, the outcome was likely to be no more than an air-clearing fist fight or exchange of musket fire.

But the situation in Europe was to shatter the Canadian calm. By 1689, Britain and France had emerged as the ranking expansionist powers. Each nation envied the other's holdings and feared its power and prestige. The question of who was to be the more powerful and the wealthier had ultimately to be settled. Beginning in that year of 1689, they squared off against each other in a series of four wars to hammer out the issue.

We shall see the Canadian results of those wars in a future chapter.

Chapter Three

Eastward the Indian Ocean

IN SEPTEMBER OF 1599, a group of 125 businessmen assembled in London for the purpose of trading with countries bordering the Indian Ocean. Sixteen months later, on December 31, 1600, as one of her final official acts of the year, an aging Queen Elizabeth granted their newborn company a charter. Calling the venture "The Governor and Company of Merchants of London trading into the East Indies," she bestowed on it the sole British trading rights with all countries lying east of the Cape of Good Hope, designating that any non-company adventurers who intruded on the preserve would risk forfeiture of their ships.

Thus was born Britain's East India Company.

It was a puny infant at birth, involving an investment of little more than thirty thousand pounds by its backers, but it was destined to evolve into a commercial goliath. In time, it would command hundreds of ships, employ seamen, executives, and clerks by the thousands, and protect its interests not only with British troops but with battalions of its own European and native soldiers. It would give eighteenth-century history one of its most significant and colorful figures: the ambitious, efficient, and adventurous Robert Clive. For more than a century, after it had firmly established itself, it would govern vast stretches of the great triangular peninsula occupied by India on the underbelly of Asia, at last surrendering its authority to the Crown in 1858. While there, its representatives (many of them living like potentates) would build schools, hospitals, and roads, study the nation's culture and language, advise and coerce local princes, subjugate masses of the population, and set the tone for the Crown rule that would follow and extend into the middle of the twentieth century.

When the company sent its first ships around the Cape of Good Hope, it had two destinations in mind. The first was India itself, and the second was the complex of Indonesian islands lying in the little seas (the Flores, Timor, Java, and Banda) that fashion a twisting water bridge between the Indian and Pacific oceans. It had the same business in mind for both: to put its hands on spices, pepper, raw and fine silk, saltpetre, and drugs in exchange for British woolens, base metals, silver, and manufactured goods. Incidentally, of all the products to be acquired, pepper was the most influential so far as the formation of the company was concerned. The Dutch held a monopoly on the Indonesian trade at the time and had but recently raised the price of pepper traded into England from three to eight shillings per pound, and the company officials, feeling the bite on their purses, had put the enterprise together in great part for the purpose of breaking the Dutch monopoly.

The profits from the new trade promised to be enormous (as, indeed, they ultimately proved to be), but they failed to materialize immediately. Rather, the company gave its first years to meeting, enduring, and attempting to overcome savage competition. So difficult were matters that the company had to wait until 1615 before seeing one of its ships bring a cargo home from India.

The East India Company represented the third—and latest arriving—European nation in Far Eastern waters. Already securely entrenched there were Portugal and the Netherlands. The Portuguese, with Bartholomew Diaz and Vasco Da Gama in the vanguard, had blazed the trail eastward to and beyond India, and the Dutch had followed swiftly, venturing even farther eastward until they were among the Indonesian islands and building their first trading post at Bantam on Java in 1595. Then came the Java post at Batavia (now Djakarta) and such outlying posts as those on the islands of Amboina and Banda between the Celebes and New Guinea. Not only did they establish a rich trade in the Indonesians, but they sent their skippers ranging far north to do business on the islands of Japan.

In their first Indonesian years, the Dutch did not trade under the auspices of a single company. Rather, individually financed ships were sent out, with their captains forging the nation's trade by cruelly exploiting the inhabitants. But, shortly after the British formation of the East India Company, the Dutch established a similar operation, the Dutch

East India Company, its purpose being to regulate their own spice traffic.

It was this company that angrily met the first British intrusions head-on, with the newcomers retaliating in kind. Harassment of each other's ships quickly became a commonplace occurrence. It was harassment that all too often resulted in sea battles between heavily armed merchantmen. Whenever the crews of competing ships came upon each other in port, fighting was more than likely to break out. Trading shops and warehouses were rifled and sometimes set to the torch. The opposition's cargoes were sabotaged.

The situation got so out of hand that the two companies, each to protect its own welfare, negotiated a peace treaty and an amalgamation in 1619. It was an agreement that was doomed from the start, a fact that became tragically evident in 1623, just four years later, when the Dutch governor at Amboina accused twelve English there of a conspiracy against his country's interests and had them executed.

Soon known at home as the "Amboina massacre," the incident had a consequential impact on the future of British history in Asia—in its way as much of an impact as the defeat of the Armada had on New World history. It caused the East India Company officials to throw up their hands not only in disgust but in the quiet admission—it was never made public—that the Dutch could no longer be coped with in Indonesia. Thereafter, the British concentrated on building their foothold in India, leaving the Dutch in control of Indonesia—until 1811 when the British took over at Java and Sumatra.

The historic import of the British company's decision is obvious. It marked the beginning of a chain of events whose final link would be the acquisition of one of the Empire's largest holdings.

The India to which the British came in the dawning seventeenth century consisted of what today is the Republic of India itself and sizable chunks of Kashmir and Jammu, West Pakistan, and Bangladesh (formerly East Pakistan). In all, it embraced more than 1,250,000 square miles. The country is, in our time, the home of about 500 million people, with its population expected to pass the 617 million mark by 1975. Three hundred years ago the extent of its population was unknown, but was guessed to have been around 120 million. The people, however, were as they remain today— a human complexity of farmers, herders, laborers, artisans, merchants, and intellectuals, representing six major religions and divided into social castes that have been estimated at between two and three thousand.

The nation lies along the underbelly of Asia, with its southern half forming a peninsula that juts into the Indian Ocean. To the west of the peninsula is the Arabian Sea and to the east the Bay of Bengal. The country is divided into three geographical regions, the first of which is formed by the Himalayan mountain system along its northern borders. The second is the river plains area, a fertile stretch that, running fifteen hundred miles from west to east, extends southward for two hundred miles and is washed with rich silt and melting snows from the Himalayas. The third is the Deccan, a great plateau that occupies most of peninsular India. It is sprinkled with mountains, forests, and vast stretches of open land for farming and grazing.

India is a land richly endowed for agriculture, washed as

it is by such rivers as the Ganges and the Indus, bathed by annual monsoon rainfalls, and divided in the main between wet and dry tropical and humid subtropical climates. Its variety of crops is wide, ranging from the tobacco, coffee, millet, rice, jute, tea, and peanuts that are grown along or near its coasts to the sorghum, sugar cane, wheat, cotton, and corn that flourish in its interior. Livestock runs from conventional (to the Western eye) cattle, sheep, and goats to the unusual (again, to the Western eye) water buffalo. Offshore, in both the Arabian Sea and the Bay of Bengal, mackerel and herring are plentiful.

The nation also has its fair share of metallic and non-metallic mineral resources. Those occurring in greatest quantity include bauxite, coal, gold, mica, and iron ore. Nature has been particularly generous with the last two; India currently provides about nine-tenths of the world's supply of mica and is reputed to hold the world's leading reserves of high-grade iron ore. It is less fortunate, however, in its lead and copper resources. Its greatest lack is in petroleum, cobalt, zinc, nickel ores, and phosphates. The country does have oil deposits in the Assam and Gujarat regions, but they are able to supply only a fraction of its current needs.

By the time the first of the East India Company ships put in an appearance, India could boast a history that dated back more than four thousand years, with the earliest of her civilizations flourishing some twenty-five hundred years before Christ in the Indus River valley of what is now West Pakistan. Known as the Harrapan civilization, it consisted of more than one hundred cities and towns and was crosscut with a network of canals for the transportation of goods. Its farms were served by irrigation ditches, and its fortified cities, built much of brick, were graced with heated public baths, indoor plumbing, and underground sewage systems. Its people knew how to read, write, weigh, and make measurements.

Sometime around 1800 B.C., the Harrapan civilization disappeared—literally vanished, the shifting earth of the passing centuries covering its cities over so completely that they were not seen again until an archaeological team stumbled upon them in 1922. The fate that befell the people there is the cause of some disagreement among historians. One view holds that they were perhaps the victims of catastrophic floods or some mighty social or economic upheaval. Another —pretty much doubted—theorizes that they may have been slaughtered by some advance group of Aryans, the warlike, fair-skinned shepherd tribesmen who came down through the Himalayas to India from central Asia in about 1500 B.C. The actual reason for the Harrapan disappearance remains a mystery to this day.

The long path to modern India can be traced to the Aryans, whose name comes from the Sanskrit word meaning "lords of the land." Shortly after arriving in the northern regions, they pushed on a modest distance south and came upon a city-dwelling, dark-skinned race of merchants and traders called the Dravidians. Some Dravidians remained to join and serve the Aryans, but many more fled down to peninsular India and became the ancestors of today's Indians. The Aryans remained in power for perhaps seven centuries and, though they did not conquer all of the country, they spread their influence everywhere. Throughout their reign, they insisted that strict social and economic barriers be maintained between themselves and the Dravidians. The practice marked the start of the complicated caste system that was to become such an Indian characteristic.

Long before the arrival of the Aryans, most Indians had learned to live in villages. Each settlement, surrounded by farming land, was governed by a chief, or, as his fellow townsmen called him, a "headsman." He inherited or was elected to his position, and in his hands was the final say on all matters of village life—from the observance and maintenance of customs to the arbitration of legal and commercial disputes and the approval of impending marriages. Sometime after 1000 B.C., many of the villages began developing into city-kingdoms, with their headsmen graduating into rich and mighty rajahs, or kings. In time, the sprawling peninsula was occupied from one end to the other by such kingdoms. Although many were taken over by invaders or larger kingdoms from time to time, they invariably managed to outlive their conquerors and emerge intact, effectively preventing any lasting unification of the country until our own century. As we shall see in a later chapter, even when the British were dominant there, they did not administer the entire nation. There were at the time, in fact, two nations—British India and a collection of several large independent kingdoms.

Beginning with the Aryans, India's history much concerns itself with the attempted and sometimes momentarily successful conquest of these kingdoms. Alexander the Great invaded the northwest area in 326 B.C. and remained there briefly. Later—between two hundred and three hundred years before the birth of Christ—the Maurya Empire with its array of petty states and principalities took shape and spread itself throughout great sections of the country and the lands adjoining it. Scythian invaders arrived in northern India in about A.D. 120 and established the Kushan dynasty there, a succession of kings that was eventually replaced by the Gupta dynasty, which ruled the northern regions from approximately A.D. 300 to around A.D. 500.

From A.D. 450 until the early sixteenth century, India was the scene of one foreign intrusion after the other. The Huns were the first to arrive, pressing in from central Asia. Then came the Moslems from the northwest in the eighth and eleventh centuries, and then the Tartars in the late fourteenth century. Finally, in 1526, a little less than forty years after Bartholomew Diaz succeeded in rounding the Cape of Good Hope, a Moslem ruler named Babar moved into India from his kingdom in Afghanistan and conquered the lands ruled by the sultan of Delhi. On the basis of this victory, he founded the greatest of all the Indian empires, the Mogul Empire. By the time its expansion was complete, its provinces and affiliated kingdoms extended all the way south across the river plains and down through the Deccan to within a few miles of the peninsula's Indian Ocean tip.

It was an empire that was at its peak when the first East India Company ships appeared on the horizon.

The company's initial Indian voyages—all conducted before 1615—failed to produce a single homeward-bound cargo. What they amounted to was a continuing, and ultimately successful, series of attempts to establish, in the eye of fierce

Portuguese competition, a beachhead from which future trade efforts could be launched.

The first company ship to reach India was the *Hector,* commanded by William Hawkins, who made port on the west side of the peninsula, at Surat on the Gulf of Cambay, which lies just a few miles north of present-day Bombay. He traveled deep inland by caravan to the city of Agra, there to seek a trade agreement with Jahangir, Babar's great-grandson and the currently reigning Mogul emperor. The two became close friends, but no trade concessions were forthcoming, for the Portuguese were already making growling noises about the newcomer, and Jahangir was not eager to rile them.

A second probe, sent out in 1611, might have resulted in a cargo had not the Portuguese at Surat undermined the British by threatening revenge on local officials who dared deal with them and by passing around stories that the newcomers were greedy, not to be trusted, and contemptuous of Indian beliefs. The year, however, brought some success over on the eastern side of the peninsula. There, at Masulipatam, which is situated about midway between today's Calcutta and the peninsula's southern tip, the company managed to secure enough local cooperation to get a trading post under way.

The western effort achieved its first success in the following year when two East India merchantmen appeared off Surat and were promptly attacked by a larger force of Portuguese vessels. The British responded with a cannon fire that was as accurate as that leveled against the Armada and sent the attackers fleeing. Company prestige surged in the eyes of the native onlookers, and word of the victory spread inland to Jahangir. The result: the admiring emperor issued an edict granting the newcomers the right to do commerce at Surat; immediately, a trading post was set up in a rented building there. Three years later, after yet another naval skirmish with the Portuguese, the company had its first Indian cargo on the way home and Britain had ensconced its first ambassador in the court of Jahangir.

The company efficiently capitalized on these initial successes. It steadily added ships to its fleet until, in 1614, they numbered twenty-four, and spent the years between 1611 and 1619 establishing trading posts—they were called "factories" at the time—on both the west and east coasts. In the west, a post went in at Broach, just to the north of Surat on the Gulf of Cambay, and another some miles northward in the interior at the city of Ahmadabad. Over east, one took shape at Pettapoli. Inland, one was built at Agra. Later years saw such construction begin at Bombay in the west and at Armagoan, Cuddalore, Cuttack, and Madras in the east. The latter, located on what is called the Coromandel Coast, became the company's first Bay of Bengal headquarters, while Bombay came to serve in that capacity over on the Arabian Sea.

The establishment of trading posts—armed, warehoused, and their offices staffed with supervisors, agents, clerks and their families—continued unabated throughout the century, with the company persistently on the lookout for good natural harbors, a resource with which the rugged peninsula coastlines are poorly endowed. By century's end, a company representative assigned to the job of putting in a settlement on the Bay of Bengal's northern shores laid the foundations for present-day Calcutta. That city soon joined Bombay and Madras as a company headquarters. All were strategically located to take the best advantage of the Indian trade.

With the coming of the British, Portuguese influence in India began to diminish. The little nation's power there had depended on its control of the surrounding waters, and now the take-over by a superior maritime country proved too much for it. Furthermore, its fall was assisted in the latter half of the century by the French and the Dutch with their superb ships. In 1664, the French established the Compagnie de Indes Orientales and secured Mogul permission to found trading posts at Surat, Pondicherry, Masulipatam, Balasore, Kasimbazar, Calicut, and Mahe. At about the same time, the Dutch, rich from their Indonesian spice trade but still wanting a slice of the India pie, wrested the offshore island of Ceylon from the Portuguese and even established a colony on the Cape of Good Hope along the route to the Far East. In the teeth of such competition—and bothered by the lesser Indian Ocean trading efforts of the Swedes and the Danes— Portugal by the first years of the eighteenth century had dwindled to a mere shadow of her former self in India. Her day was done.

Of the European powers trading in India early in the new century, Britain and France were the most powerful. But, in sharp contrast to the brawling and skirmishing that broke out whenever they met in faraway Canada, they worked quite peaceably alongside each other in their Indian factories, for the soundest of reasons.

Their representatives in India were adventurers, willing

to leave the security of home for an overseas opportunity, but they were not the free-booting frontiersmen that Canada attracted. Rather, they were sophisticated businessmen who were keenly aware that a few years of uninterrupted work could earn them a fortune that would last a lifetime or more. Through their hands daily passed a king's ransom in cargoes; for the British, each homeward-bound ship carried about fifty thousand pounds' worth of goods, or about twenty thousand pounds more than the original investment made by the company's founders. There was room for shrewd, ambitious heads to advance within either company, and there was room for anyone of entrepreneurial bent to rake in a profit on the side. Many Britishers who went out to India as company clerks or agents ended up owning their own ships and conducting a nice trade of their own. Further, even though the climate was sweltering and the native customs strange, life was comfortable. Employees and their families lived in ease with the help of meagerly paid Indian servants. Some attained such wealth that they were able to take on the life-style of kings, settling themselves in mansions that were akin to palaces.

With such opportunities at hand, no one wanted to see the companies at each other's throats. Trouble could only interfere with profits and interrupt the personal march to advancement and great wealth.

It was a peace, however, that the unfolding political situation in Europe would not allow to endure for long. As was pointed out at the close of the Canadian chapter, Britain and France had emerged as the leading overseas powers by the late seventeenth century. In a series of four wars between

Chapter Four

South Down the Pacific

LOCATED FAR TO the east and south of India, the island continent of Australia lay long neglected between the Indian and Pacific oceans. The area of this distant land, including that of the triangular island of Tasmania off its southeast coast, nearly equals the area of the forty-eight states of the continental United States, but no western man chanced upon it until the start of the seventeenth century, long after explorers had extended the horizons to the New World. And the first Europeans to glimpse the Australian coasts said that the place was worthless and dangerous, a good landfall to avoid.

They had a point, for much of Australia is dry, unproductive desert, owing to the fact that despite its size—fourteen hundred miles long by two thousand miles wide—the island continent has few mountains to precipitate rainfall. A tableland, rising no more than two thousand feet above sea level, dominates Western Australia and extends northward as far as the Gulf of Carpentaria. Throughout the flatland's vast expanse, nature has never permitted the formation of permanent lake and river systems.

But on the east side of Carpentaria there is a change in terrain. Here, starting with the Cape York Peninsula and extending south along a course parallel with Australia's bulging east coast, are mountains. They are not high—few climb above the five-thousand-foot mark—but they are the continent's most significant geographic feature, for they provide a watershed. Annual rainfall on the Cape York Peninsula exceeds sixty inches and in some areas even reaches one hundred inches, blanketing much of the peninsula with a verdant tropical rain forest. Australia's chief river systems, with valleys of fertile soil, lie on either side of the southward-running mountain system, which is known as the Great Dividing Range. Its water benefits made possible the continent's early settlements by western man, but the natural barrier of its heights, like that of North America's Allegheny chain, long blocked his advance into the interior.

Geologically, the 24,450-square-mile Tasmania, though separated from the mainland by Bass Strait, is considered an extension of the Great Dividing Range. With an annual rainfall equaling that of the Cape York Peninsula, much of the island is forested. Its mountain valleys provide rich pastures for grazing. Its soil is excellent for crops.

East of Australia, some twelve hundred miles across the wind-whipped Tasman Sea, another mountain range forms the spine of the two major islands of New Zealand. Aligned

generally southwest-northeast, and with a tip pointing northwest like a crooked finger, North Island and South Island,
together with their small offshore islands, add up to an area
of 103,736 square miles. Though nearly equal in size, the
two islands are quite distinct one from the other. North
Island lies low to the sea, but is cut by steep hills and ridges.
South Island, though of a mountainous, alpine aspect, contains more open land than its northern sister. On South
Island, Mount Cook rises to a height of 12,349 feet. The
southern coast of South Island is indented with spectacular,
glacier-carved fjords.

Stone Age tribes populated both Australia and New Zealand eons ago, with the Aborigines finally dominating Australia while the Maoris won New Zealand for themselves.

Anthropologists class the Maoris as Polynesians, that great
race of brown people who are believed to have originated
somewhere in southeast Asia and who traveled out to join
the darker-skinned Melanesians in populating the entire
South Pacific. But the beginnings of the Aborigines are unknown and continue to bewilder anthropologists to this day.
A nomadic, hunting and food-gathering people who differ
from the Polynesians and Melanesians in many physical
characteristics, they have been classified as a separate race—
Australoid.

They may have originated in Australia itself, but a number of anthropologists think that unlikely, saying that the
Aborigines probably came from inland Asia. They base their
belief on similarities they have noted between certain Aboriginal customs and those practiced by several hill tribes in
far northern India. They theorize that the black natives of

Tasmania at one time occupied Australia and then fled in the face of invaders. Though no native Tasmanians survive today, they are known to have differed from the Aborigines in customs and in physical features.

The history of the Maoris, on the other hand, is easier to trace. According to their own legends, they came ashore at the New Zealand islands in what would be A.D. 1350 by Western dating, arriving there after a journey south from Tahiti. A fierce people with tattooed faces and a taste for human flesh, they liquidated the original New Zealanders. No clue to the appearance of the original inhabitants was left behind.

Long before the birth of Christ, Greek philosophers developed the theory that the Southern Hemisphere was dominated by a giant continent. The Greeks reasoned that such a continent had to exist to balance the known lands of the Northern Hemisphere and thus hold the world upright. In time, the theoretical continent became known as Terra Australis, or South Land, and imaginative cartographers of the day drew it into their maps, endowing it with long peninsulas that extended toward the equator. They drew one such peninsula—a bulging thing—between the latitudes bordering what was to be Australia and called it Patalis Regio.

Since man gained no hard facts with which to dispute the whole concept, the Greek notion stayed alive for nearly two thousand years. Even in 1601, when Portuguese navigator Manuel Godhino de Eradia reported sighting land south of New Guinea, he seemed only to confirm the theory. Historians cannot be certain if he saw the Australian mainland or just some offshore island, and Spain's Luiz Vaes de Torres did little to clear up the situation when, in 1606, he sailed through the ninety-five-mile-wide strait that lies between New Guinea and the Cape York Peninsula and that now bears his name. He did not bother to note in detail the features of the land that lay to his south.

The distinction of being the first Westerner to land at Australia goes to the Dutch navigator William Jansz. Several months after the Torres voyage, he sailed eastward from his country's Indonesian spice ports and nosed into the Gulf of Carpentaria. He went ashore, but, unfortunately, ran into a band of hostile natives who unhesitantly attacked his crew and killed several of his men. He made his way back to Java, where he warned his fellow Netherlanders to stay clear of the gulf area. His expedition might have done much to begin replacing the ancient Greek theory with solid fact, but his warning succeeded only in delaying further Australian exploration for years to come. Much future discovery there was to be the result of accident, sometimes horrible accident.

To reach their Indonesian outposts, Dutch skippers had learned to hold a course in high latitudes long after rounding the Cape of Good Hope. The prevailing westerlies sped the tall square riggers eastward for more than three thousand miles before it was time to turn northward and make port. In 1616, Captain Dirk Hartog held his eastward run too long and came upon a strange coast. He located a sheltered bay, went ashore at an island in it, and put up a plaque to mark the event before sailing on. By accident, he had discovered Shark Bay on western Australia's central coast.

His was a lucky accident, for he made his landfall in daylight. Not so fortunate was the ship *Batavia,* which blundered up to the west Australian coast on a June night in 1629 while carrying emigrants to Indonesia. A more unlucky mistake can hardly be imagined.

The big ship, heavy with cargo and baggage, went aground on an offshore island. With more than two hundred passengers and crew cast up on a waterless, treeless beach, Captain François Pelsart set sail at once in a ship's boat to bring help before the *Batavia*'s provisions gave out. As soon as he departed, most of the crew mutinied and set to work solving the supply shortage by massacring 125 passengers. Forty-seven survived to set up an armed camp on a neighboring island, where they held the mutineers at bay until Pelsart, who had managed a remarkable two-thousand-mile open-boat voyage to Java, appeared with a rescue ship.

Most of the mutineers were hanged, but two, whose guilt was in doubt, were left on the island when the survivors sailed away. The fate of the pair, Australia's first unwilling settlers, is unknown. Two hundred years would pass before men willingly housed themselves on the western shores of the continent.

For more than a decade following the *Batavia* disaster, the Dutch ignored Australia, concentrating on their Indonesian holdings. But in 1642, the energetic Antony van Diemen, the governor-general of Java, sent Abel J. Tasman south to determine the extent of the little-known land mass. Tasman, who had earlier explored the Philippine coasts for the Dutch, sailed along the underbelly of Australia and destroyed once and for all the theory that it was part of a great southern continent. He landed on an island which he named Van

Diemen's Land (now Tasmania) and then ventured far west to discover New Zealand before turning back to Java.

In a second voyage—made in 1644—Tasman explored some one thousand miles of Australia's northwest coast in a vain search for timber and spices. His unhappy report so dampened Netherlands enthusiasm that the Dutch East Indies Company quietly decreed it would be best if Australia remained an uninvestigated mystery so that competing nations would not be able to use it at a later date to undermine Dutch Pacific influence.

The short-sighted policy foretold the end of Dutch ascendancy in the East, but other world powers were as yet too preoccupied with other interests and problems to take up the unfinished task of Australian exploration. In 1688, however, the Englishman William Dampier, one of history's strangest pirates, cruised for several months along the continent's west coast and then returned to London to write a book about the voyage, *New Voyage Around the World,* that, oddly, contained more about flora and fauna than about boarding tactics and broadsides. When published, it attracted widespread interest and prompted the Admiralty in 1699 to send out an expedition under Dampier's command to investigate further. In *New Voyage,* the pirate whose real interest in life was nature study had written that ships could reach Australia from east to west around Cape Horn in Magellan's wake as well as by the traditional west-east route via the Cape of Good Hope. The Admiralty instructed him to put his theory to the test, but sent him out in the wrong season.

The expedition, consisting of two rotting ships and free-booting crews, was destined for failure, even though it reached Australia, probed the northern coast of New Guinea, and discovered the island of New Britain. Both ships, no match for the wild weather encountered and for the temper of the men sailing them, broke up, with the second of their number going down off Ascension Island in the Atlantic on the return home. Dampier was brought back to England aboard a man-of-war in 1701, stood court martial for marooning a mutinous crewman, and, despite the fact that he seemed to be happier wielding a pen or a butterfly net than a cutlass, returned to piracy. The experience of his second voyage discouraged the British from taking another look at Australia for well over half a century.

When the Lords of the Admiralty next sent an expedition to the far side of the world, the ship was sound, its crew well chosen, and its skipper, Captain James Cook, one of the most capable seamen of his day.

Between 1768 and his death on February 14, 1779, at the hands of Hawaiian natives, Cook made three voyages to the Pacific aboard the coaling bark *Endeavor*. On these journeys, he pushed deep into southern waters in search of the legendary continent of Terra Australis; visited the eastern and northern coasts of Australia; discovered the Society Islands, the Hawaiians* (which he christened the Sandwich Islands in honor of Lord Sandwich, then chief of the Admiralty), and such smaller groups as the Cook (also known as the Hervey) Archipelago; proved that New Zealand con-

---

* It is perhaps more appropriate to use the word "re-discovered" in connection with the Hawaiian Islands, for they are thought to have been first sighted by Juan Gaetano of Spain in 1555 and then subsequently forgotten.

sisted of islands and was not an outcropping of Terra Australis; and ventured as far north as the Aleutians, the Alaskan coast, and the Bering Strait.

In his search for Terra Australis, Cook made three probes into Antarctic waters, one of them coming to within two hundred miles of the Antarctic land mass. He demonstrated that the Greek theory, though romantic, was a mistaken notion and that no giant southern continent existed—at least, not within habitable climes and certainly not of the proportions envisioned by the Greeks. The land mass of Antarctica—huge in itself, but a dwarf when compared with the Terra Australis concept—was to wait for discovery until well into the nineteenth century.

As far as Australia and New Zealand are concerned, Cook's first voyage (1768–1771) held the greatest significance. After establishing a scientific station at Tahiti from which a rare transit of the planet Venus across the sun could be studied, he sailed the *Endeavor* southwest, sighted New Zealand, and circumnavigated it, proving it to be two separate islands. Then, when an attempt to befriend the Maoris proved fruitless, he continued southwest, his intention now to locate Tasmania. A howling storm, however, blew him off course, and his next landfall was the east coast of Australia.

No European had hitherto looked on these shores, and so Cook cruised slowly northward, painstakingly charting all he saw until he came to a large natural harbor, where he dropped anchor. Coming ashore, he found himself confronted by a group of natives with upraised spears, but a few rifle shots aimed above their heads sent them running.

Joseph Banks, the expedition's chief scientist, soon stumbled upon scores of plants never catalogued before, and at his suggestion, Cook named the shelter Botany Bay. Continuing north, Cook somehow missed another large anchorage, the bay that now serves Sydney's port. Generally, however, his charts of the eastern coast have been found to be remarkably complete and accurate, typical of all his work.

The passing land reminded Cook of Wales, and though he had first called his discovery New Holland in recognition of earlier Dutch navigators, he now changed the name to New South Wales. Along the continent's northeastern face, he encountered what was to become known as the Great Barrier Reef, a 1,250-mile stretch of coral reef. The *Endeavor* went aground on the coral at one point, but Cook backed her off, made repairs on her hull, sailed past the obstacle, and beat his way to Java. In June of 1771, he completed his voyage with a welcome English landfall.

The tales of discovery and adventure brought home by the *Endeavor*'s crew helped to take British minds, for the moment at least, from the troubles with the American colonies. Discontent there was growing stronger by the day, and while Cook was on his second voyage, the Revolutionary War broke out. And during his third voyage, when he was clubbed to death while trying to recapture a ship's boat stolen by Hawaiian natives, the war was four years old.

The Revolution, fought and won in a distant hemisphere, sealed Australia's destiny. For years, Britain had been sending her convicted robbers, thieves, confidence men, pickpockets, rabble rousers, and prostitutes to America as forced laborers. While the mother country thus rid herself of the unwanted of her population, the New World colonies gained the cheapest of workers, but the Revolution brought this convenient practice to an end. Now a new overseas dumping ground had to be found, and Banks suggested that far-away Botany Bay might prove an ideal site for a penal colony. His idea lay dormant until 1786 when the Home Secretary, Lord Sydney, desperate over the crowded conditions in English jails, finally took action. He drew up the orders for transportation of convicts to the southeastern Australian coast, to what was to be called the New South Wales Colony.

At the time, England's ruling class looked upon the indigent poor as a menace, and so the smallest offense by any of their number could earn transportation to the Pacific. A starving and aged soldier was sent there for stealing a broom. Several children were transported for handkerchief theft. It is true that many hardened criminals were marched in chains aboard the Australia-bound ships, but just as many others could not qualify at all as genuine lawbreakers, not even by the most meager of criteria. At least 475 laborers were once banished for suggesting that their employers were not paying them enough to feed their families. It was of these persecuted and debased human beings that Australia's first white population was made.

While the prisoners were a mixed lot, the men sent to guard them in the new colony were, pretty universally, a disreputable crew. Military regiments were scoured for recruits to serve in what was called the New South Wales Corps, but no one with an ounce of promise wished to abandon his unit for the privilege of overseeing convicts while they built cabins and planted crops. With rare exceptions, it was the inept, the unruly, the drunken, and the lazy who volunteered. The widespread comment that the guards and not the prisoners should have worn the chains on the outbound voyage was more than an idle joke.

The first contingent of transport ships to arrive in New South Wales Colony docked at Botany Bay on January 18, 1788, under the command of Captain Arthur Phillip. Eight days later, unimpressed with the surrounding sun-baked coast, he took the ships out again and moved them north to the large bay that one day would serve the city of Sydney. Phillip christened it Port Jackson and, late in the evening of January 26, he gathered his guards and convicts in a grove of gum trees, had his commission as governor of the new colony read aloud, ordered three cheers for the king, and issued a pint of rum to every man and a half-pint to every woman. Colonization of Australia had begun.

Under Phillip, the colony should have had a good start. He was a capable man, vested with absolute power over the community, and blessed with the good sense to use it well. But he was in for trouble, and his problem was that he had few good men at hand. Many of the prisoners, poorly treated on the voyage, were too ill or too weak for work. And the guards, who looked upon the prisoners as their labor force, adroitly sidestepped all physical work. Finally, as if the hazards posed by inefficient personnel were not enough, the land around the harbor proved too poor to nurture freshly planted crops. The colony tottered on the brink of disaster during its first months.

Matters seemed to improve when rich bottom land was located in the river valleys running up to the nearby mountains, and several guards were sent there to establish farms. But the improvement was only temporary, the forerunner of a problem that was to endure for years to come. The guards took prisoners with them as indentured workers; "slaves" is probably the more apt term, for the convicts received little more in pay than was necessary to keep them alive. The pay was rum—and rum was to be the Australian problem that wouldn't go away.

It was a problem that even the capable Phillip could not solve. Rum became currency, a currency that the guards soon controlled and that was more than welcome in a place where misery and homesickness were rife. Those with stills produced so much of the stuff that, before long, half the colony was in their debt. The guards acquired so much influence and power through the illegal liquor trade that they could bribe anyone, official and prisoner alike, to get their way in any matter. Instead of the New South Wales Corps, the guards soon became known as the "Rum Corps."

Despite the problem, Phillip did manage to establish enough farms to support the colony, but ill health forced him to resign in 1792. There followed a procession of inept governors, none able to break the tyranny of the Rum Corps.

The next able man to govern the New South Wales Colony was Colonel Lachlan Macquarie, who arrived in 1809. Armed with his own regiment—the Seventy-Third—he had sufficient muscle to break the back of the Rum Corps, a job that he did quickly and efficiently. Though disbanded, the group continued to cause trouble because most of its members elected to remain in the colony and exert their influence as landowners and free men. The illegal rum trade, however, was snuffed out.

Macquarie served until 1821, launching schools, building hospitals, bridges, and roads, and incurring the wrath of those who came to the colony as free men. The exclusionists, as they were called, wanted the right to hold land and public office denied to those who had been sent to Australia as convicts, but who had subsequently earned their freedom. The former convicts—dubbed emancipists—increased in number each year, thanks to governmental pardon or completion of their sentences, and Macquarie recognized that they held the best promise for the colony's growth. He made many friends among them, put some in charge of his public works projects, and often entertained their leaders at dinner parties in his home—a practice which outraged the exclusionists more than anything else.

Despite the conflict between the two factions, a conflict that would long be a thorn in Australia's side, the colony in New South Wales expanded during the Macquarie years. In 1813, the Blue Mountains just west of the Sydney harbor settlement—the most rugged of the Great Dividing Range —were finally crossed and the fertile Bathurst Plains were opened for settlement. Other expeditions followed, among them the initial investigations of the upper tributaries of the Murray River, Australia's largest.

The early nineteenth century not only brought the capable Macquarie to Australia, but also marked the beginning development of Tasmania and New Zealand.

Of the two, the former's early colonial history was by far the more turbulent. In 1803, six years before Macquarie's arrival at the Sydney settlement, a penal colony was established at Tasmania for Britain's worst criminals. Its administration was entrusted to a succession of Australian governors, but the practice was to send a lieutenant governor there and then to ignore the place altogether. As a consequence, the little island was poorly supervised and, with its stick- and wattle-hovel town of Hobart, became a hell on earth. Since the first convict arrivals were inadequately supplied, their guards had no choice but to turn them loose on the land to fend for themselves. Brutal men to begin with, many degenerated to savagery as they roamed the forested mountains for game. They took to murdering natives and butchering them to feed their dogs, and went from there to raping native women and torturing their menfolk for the sport of it. These atrocities so infuriated the indigenous population that soon no white men could wander far from Hobart and hope to remain alive.

As for Hobart, it had its own array of outrages. Drunken fighting was an everyday occurrence. Women were sold at auction in the streets. The town was ruled by harsh magistrates, and five hundred lashes—certain death—was not an uncommon punishment for a crime as minor as the theft of a cheap watch. Court witnesses were tortured until they gave evidence pleasing to the magistrates. Anyone who dared to rebel at such tactics was publicly flogged.

The whole abysmal situation at Tasmania was to persist well into the nineteenth century, until free settlers finally began to outnumber and replace the convicts. In the meantime—in the mid-1820s—the atrocities done to the original population brought on open warfare. It ended with the liquidation of all Tasmanians.

The initial settlement of New Zealand by whites had little deliberate design to it, for the government at London long chose to ignore the two islands after Cook had claimed them for the Crown during his 1769 voyage. Parliament was at first not interested in them as points of foreign exploitation and then was content with its Australian penal colony. The result: New Zealand's first settlers turned out to be runaway sailors who made their way there from British warships and merchantmen. They arrived as early as 1790 and, by the turn of the century, were housed in permanent settlements and compounds along the coast.

But, as had happened elsewhere and as would happen throughout the history of colonial development, trouble festered between the Maoris and the newcomers. It was a trouble, consisting of raids and ambushes on both sides of the fence, that worsened as more and more Europeans were attracted to the thriving seal and whaling industry then taking shape in the South Pacific. England's only reaction to all the friction in New Zealand was to appoint one James Busby to represent the interest of British subjects there. Even when a brief but sharply fought war (1834–1835) broke out with the Maoris, the mother country did not intervene.

Busby's appointment, however, proved to be a fortunate one. In 1835, complicating the Maori situation, a French adventurer named de Thierry arrived and declared himself king of New Zealand. Busby used this new foreign threat to unite the Maori chieftains with him and drive the intruder out. The action led to British negotiations for peace and the signing, on February 6, 1840, of the Waitangi Treaty by fifty chieftains. Later, five hundred signatures were collected, each consisting of a sketch of the chief's distinctive facial tattoo.

The treaty ceded New Zealand sovereignty to Queen Victoria and made the possession a dependency of the colonial government in Australia. The queen, in turn, agreed to protect the natives and honor their property rights. Britain was committed to her two faraway islands at last, and the designation of New Zealand as a separate Crown colony passed Parliament on May 3, 1841.

As mid-century approached, Britain's three principal South Pacific possessions were well settled, with Australia and Tasmania steadily losing their prison-colony look. More and more free men were arriving and the population in Australia alone had risen from ten thousand in 1809 to more than sixty thousand. And, thanks to the crossing of the Great Dividing Range in 1813, the sprawling inland area was now available for future farming and grazing.

But that is a story that belongs to a later chapter. It belongs to the British lion as he stands in the noonday of his colonial development. For one aspect of the future—grazing—was to be responsible for Australia's greatest growth.

Part Two

The Lion at Noon

Chapter Five

The Lion in the West

In 1775—166 years after the first of their number had been founded at Jamestown—Britain's Atlantic seaboard colonies in the New World rebelled against the increasingly tyrannical authority of London. Four years later, with the surrender of General Charles Cornwallis at Yorktown, the colonies emerged as an independent federation of states.

The First British Empire was at an end—the victim of unwise policies at home and a tradition of self-rule that had been born on the Atlantic seaboard with the Mayflower Compact and had grown steadily ever since.

But, though her prestige was badly mauled, her hold on the New World was far from lost. Eastward into the Atlantic, she still occupied—as she had done since 1612—the Bermuda Islands. To the south, English-speaking colonists were to be found throughout the Caribbean area, that former

83

Spanish stronghold. Arriving at St. Kitts-Nevis and Anguilla Islands in the Leeward chain as early as 1623 and at Barbados in 1627, they had come in force during the Puritan Migration of 1629–1640, settling at Montserrat in 1632; Antigua, Barbuda, and Redonda in the Leewards in 1633; and at British Honduras far to the west on the Central American coast in 1638. From there, they had spread to the Bahamas (1649), Jamaica (1655), the Virgin Islands (1666), the Caymans (1670), Tobago (1763), and Dominica, Grenada, and St. Vincent in the Windwards group (1763). Now, at the close of the American Revolution, they comprised one of the richest and most powerful groups in the Caribbean, annually producing for domestic consumption and export a wide variety of crops ranging from sugar cane and tobacco to coffee, bananas, pineapples, and grapefruit. The next years would see a further extension of their influence. Under the British banner would come the Turks and Caicos islands (1799), Trinidad (1802), British Guiana on the northern coast of South America (1814), and St. Lucia in the Windwards (1814).

And to the north lay Canada, stretching westward from the Atlantic to the Pacific and northward into the Arctic Circle from the Great Lakes. It was in this sprawling wilderness that Britain was to begin building her Second Empire.

Long before the building of the Second Empire could start, Britain had to wrest Canada from the grasp of the French. It was a process that, getting underway almost one hundred years before the American Revolution, was to require almost three-quarters of a century to run its full course. It was to be a time of bloody wars and periods of restless peace, for France, with its overseas investors long fattening on the profits from Canadian furs, was to relinquish its hold with an understandable reluctance.

Ownership of the vast property was decided by the New World fighting in those four wars of the seventeenth and eighteenth centuries in which Britain and France, by then two of the most formidable of overseas landlords, sought to settle the issue of which was to be the more powerful.

The first of the four (the War of the Palatinate) was known in the New World as King William's War. At its end, neither side had any new territory and, in the main, it consisted of little more than a number of minor skirmishes, bloody though they were. The French, accompanied by Indian allies, attacked and burned the small settlement at Schenectady, New York, and then sent the Indians against the Massachusetts town of Haverhill. Enraged, the British retaliated immediately, striking out from Maine to seize Port Royal (now Annapolis Royal) on Nova Scotia's Bay of Fundy coast. Almost simultaneously, an attack was aimed at Quebec, but was turned back by defenders there. The Treaty of Ryswick brought a peace that lasted five years and gave Port Royal back to France.

The second war (in Europe, the War of the Spanish Succession) broke out in 1702, ran until 1713, and was dubbed Queen Anne's War in the Americas. It was marked by another assault on Quebec, which ended disastrously for the British when their troop-carrying ships were wrecked en route. A French-Indian force massacred the colonists at Deerfield, Massachusetts, and put the little town to the torch.

The British stormed north to Port Royal and again captured the town. This time, with the Treaty of Utrecht, they managed to keep the place and with it much of the province of Nova Scotia, which had previously been known as Acadia.

The Utrecht agreement put the British and French at peace for thirty-one years. The quiet was broken between 1744 and 1748 by the War of the Austrian Succession. To the British colonists, it was King George's War and, aside from border skirmishes, it centered on Cape Breton Island in the Gulf of St. Lawrence. The French used the island as a naval base and as a jumping-off spot for raids south into British territory. Plainly, it had to be taken if the raids were to be forestalled, and a colonial force of several thousand men marched on its capital settlement, the highly fortified Louisbourg. With an assist from a British flotilla, they put the stronghold under a successful six-weeks siege, only to see it returned to the French by the Treaty of Aix-la-Chapelle. For it, however, the British regained Madras, which they had dropped to the French in India during the fighting.

Despite the trio of wars, the power struggle between Britain and France seemed no closer to resolution than it was at the start of hostilities fifty-nine years earlier. But France was beginning to show some chinks in her New World armor. Though such explorers as Marquette, Joliet, and La Salle had given her claim to the lands on both sides of the Mississippi River all the way south to the Gulf of Mexico, she had never been much of a colonizer and so had not populated her holdings to any degree through the decades. As always, her principal settlements were sprinkled around the Gulf of St. Lawrence and along the St. Lawrence River, with the seemingly endless territory to the west, to the north, and to the south for a distance down the Mississippi dotted only with forts and remote trading posts. Consequently, when the fourth of the wars erupted in 1755, she soon found her forces in the Americas stretched too thin and without the facilities to keep them adequately supplied.

This new outbreak got its start in the Ohio Valley and was called the French and Indian War. From Ohio (with an assist from India, where the East India Company and the Compagnie de Indes Orientales were squaring off against each other in the struggles of the Mogul Empire), the fighting spread to Europe and evolved into the Seven Years War. By the time it was done, French power was at last shattered in Europe, in India, and in the Americas.

A squabble over land rights west of the Appalachians caused the war. When the French built a string of forts there to protect their Mississippi territory from English-speaking settlers, the colonial British argued that several had been put up on lands belonging to them and proceeded to drive the French out. At first, up against the brilliant Marquis Louis Joseph de Montcalm de Saint Veran, they were beaten at every turn of the road. A young George Washington was mauled at Fort Necessity and an aging General Edward Braddock died with most of his troops in an ambush near Fort Duquesne. A shortage of supplies, however, finally forced Montcalm to retreat to defensive posts along the St. Lawrence, the strongest being the cliff-top citadel of Quebec.

With the tide of battle turning in their favor, the British overran enemy forts on Lake Ontario and along the river to

Lake Erie. Over in the Gulf of St. Lawrence, they stormed Cape Breton Island from the sea and took Louisbourg. There, a small and frail-looking army officer named James Wolfe displayed such military genius that he was assigned command of the impending assault on Montcalm's Quebec fortress, a maneuver that, if successful, was bound to break the back of the French.

Throughout the summer of 1759, Wolfe vainly lay siege to the citadel from the St. Lawrence at its base. Then, in the pre-dawn darkness of September 13, when all other strategies had failed, he led his army up a steep cliff to the Plains of Abraham, an open plateau leading to Quebec's back door. There, when the sun came up, he at last stood eye to eye with the enemy. Though surprised, Montcalm immediately mustered his troops and ordered a charge against the British. His force, consisting principally of militia and conscripts, was no match for the professional and veteran Redcoats, who drew themselves up in the traditional double-line of battle and impassively waited until the advancing French were within forty paces. Then British muskets went off in unison all along the line. The attack was stopped immediately. Ill-trained, with many of their number new to battle, the French broke and ran. Within minutes, the battle was over and Quebec was in British hands. Dead of wounds was Wolfe. Injured was Montcalm. He would linger until the following day. When he died, all French hopes for the New World were buried with him.

Montreal fell the next summer and the Treaty of Paris put an end to hostilities here and abroad in 1763. By the terms of the treaty, France handed over to Britain all of Canada, Cape

Breton Island, and the rest of Nova Scotia, along with her regions east of the Mississippi, retaining only the tiny islands of St. Pierre and Miquelon off the Newfoundland coast as fishing stations. In the West Indies, she surrendered the islands of Dominica, St. Vincent, Grenada, and Tobago. To Spain, which had been her ally in the European segment of the war, went her acreage west of the Mississippi—that vast wilderness tract which at the time was known as the Louisiana Territory and which would be restored to her during Napoleon's reign and then would be purchased by the young United States. Spain, however, had to give her Florida holding to Britain. By the time all was said and done, only two nations remained in continental North America—the mighty Britain and a now almost toothless Spain.

The award was a heady one. With colonies stretching from Hudson Bay to the Gulf of Mexico and from the Atlantic seaboard to the Mississippi, Britain literally ruled a continent. That the future could hold anything but greater national success and greater national power seemed impossible. But the fact was that she was just twelve years away from revolution and less than two decades away from the humiliation of Yorktown.

It was her misfortune to have on the throne a new king, George III. The nation, through her chartered companies, had always expanded overseas to cash in on the trade there and, in the case of America, to benefit economically from the development of the wilderness and to rid herself of unwanted segments of the homeland population. In general, her attitude toward the American colonies had been quite liberal. A great deal of self-rule had always been the tradition. She had profited from their trade and development, but, with few exceptions, she had never tried to bleed every last penny out of the holdings. Her strongest measure had been the Navigation Acts of the late seventeenth century, requiring the New World colonists to transport their goods on British ships and to import goods only through British ports, but even though she knew that they were being ignored and that a lively business in colonial smuggling had sprung up to sidestep them, she had done little to enforce the Acts, in part because of a sense of leniency, in part because her attention was diverted by other international matters, among them the French wars. Now, with George III on the throne, at the very time when wisdom was most needed, her colonial outlook was to change for the worse.

The new king wanted the American colonies to exist solely for the benefit of the mother country. He wanted to tax them heavily because he felt that they were not bearing their full share of the costs of the colonial wars. And, distrustful of such a representative body as Parliament and bloated with some grandiose ideas of how a monarch should conduct himself, he wanted everyone, at home and in the New World, to know that he was not simply a reigning king but a ruling one.

In such a mood, he appointed ministers sure to do his bidding and called for a series of strong economic measures against the New World holdings. He began with the Writs of Assistance, which were general search warrants that enforced the Navigation Acts by permitting British officials to break into any house or building in search of smuggled wares. Next came the Stamp Act, the first direct taxation ever imposed on the colonies. Then the Townshend Acts, which placed a duty on four items that the colonists could not do without—glass, paper, paint, and tea. And finally, after many colonials had reacted with increasing violence to the preceding measures, the Intolerable Acts, five in all. They closed the port of Boston to all trade until the citizenry there agreed to pay for the damage done by the Boston Tea Party; deprived the people of Massachusetts of all voice in their government and placed a British general, Thomas Gage, in charge of the colony; called for any English soldier or official charged with an American crime to be tried back home, where he would find the legal climate more friendly; demanded that the colonists quarter homeland troops in their houses; and closed the territory north of the Ohio River and east of the Mississippi to Americans and made it a part of Canada. This final provision was known as the Quebec Act. We shall hear more of it shortly.

The result: revolution broke out in the colonies south of the Canadian line in 1775 and, for all intents and purposes, ended six years later at Yorktown, though intense fighting continued in some quarters for another year. Hostilities were formally called to a halt with the Treaty of Paris in 1783.

What in the next centuries could have proved to be one of Britain's richest holdings was lost to her. The First Empire, which had reached its zenith with the close of the Seven Years War just two decades earlier, was at an end.

Now, what of Canada? What occurred within her borders throughout the years before, during, and after the Revolution?

The close of the French and Indian Wars in 1763 brought no great change in the lives of Canada's French residents, who numbered little more than sixty thousand at the time. They endured the country's change of name from New France to Canada, saw the first English-speaking governors take office, and heard the call go out for British settlers who would broaden the economic base there by putting as much emphasis on farming as on trapping and fishing, but that was about all. However, close on the heels of peace there came a royal proclamation that limited all government appointments to Protestants. It startled everyone, infuriating the Catholic French and violating the sense of fair play in many of the Protestant English. George III seemed about to be as annoying to the Canadians as the Americans.

Fortunately, the early British governors assigned to Canada were generally sympathetic to the French, and so the fruits of the proclamation did not lead to unjust treatment of the French. Then came the Quebec Act. Intended to punish the Americans, it reversed the strictures of the proclamation and allowed Roman Catholics to hold office. Immediately, the bad taste left by the proclamation was gone. Besides, by handing over the acreage north of the Ohio River and east of the Mississippi to Canada, the Act delighted the Canadians, providing them with much rich western land for development.

The Quebec Act spiked any sympathy for an American revolt that might have been raised in the northern provinces. But, even without the Act, it is doubtful that, in the end, the Canadians would have joined or supported the Americans in their fight against the mother country. They were in

economic competition with the colonies to the south, and so
why should they—as fishermen, fur trappers, farmers, and
merchants—have taken sides with their competitors?

When the southern unrest erupted into open war, the
thirteen American colonies, nevertheless, hoped that Canada
would join with them. They saw that hope killed when they
attempted an invasion of the country. The onslaught, begun
with the idea that the incoming troops would be welcomed
and would kindle the torch of revolution throughout the
North, disintegrated into a vain attack on Quebec on the
last day of 1775, followed by an equally fruitless march on
Nova Scotia in the next year. The predicted sympathy for
the American cause simply did not materialize. Canada
chose to go her own way as a loyal British holding.

However, the new republic demanded, and received, sizable Canadian concessions in the Treaty of Paris. American
fishermen gained the right to work the coastal waters of
Nova Scotia, the St. Lawrence, and Newfoundland. American trappers were admitted into vast territories that Canadian explorers had discovered and that Canadian traders
now considered their own. And to the new nation went all
the land from the Atlantic to the Mississippi and from the
Canadian border to Florida, which was ceded back to Spain,
to be held by that country for a few years more; in the vast
land grant was the property that had been taken from the
Americans by the Quebec Act.

But the outcome of the Revolution also gave Canada a
rich asset, one almost too rich to measure—the loyalist. Of
the one hundred thousand Americans who remained loyal
to their king, between thirty-five thousand and forty thou-

sand migrated north to find new homes. They settled in Nova Scotia, on Prince Edward Island, and in the area arcing east and west above Maine's border, the region that would soon become the separate colony of New Brunswick. They cleared land and established farms outside of Quebec and Montreal, providing these communities, and others, with a firm agricultural base. In the two years following the Revolution, loyalists swelled the population of the northern colonies by 50 percent. Without the influx of these stable, hard-working people, Canada's growth would have been long delayed.

With war at an end and with the arrival of all the newcomers, Canada was due for an era of prosperity and western movement. There was much curiosity and interest in the new land, resulting in a series of significant explorations. In 1786, British naval captain John Meares explored the northwest coast of the continent, retracing his route two years later to build and launch the *Northwest America,* the first ship ever to originate in what would become British Columbia. In 1789, Alexander Mackenzie led an expedition to the shores of the Arctic Ocean and, four years later, marched overland to the Pacific, becoming the first man to make a Canadian transcontinental crossing. Meanwhile, George Vancouver, who had twice sailed to the Pacific with Captain Cook, conducted a survey of the Pacific coast. His detailed work, done between 1792 and 1794, served to clinch the British claim to Canada's western shores.

While the country's external limits came better into focus during the final two decades of the eighteenth century, so did its principal internal problem—the division between its

French and British cultures, which troubles Canada to this day. The timely Quebec Act of 1774 had favored the French, but the loyalists who had arrived since were now speaking out against certain governmental approaches which had been hallmarks of French colonial administration and which now persisted in the British system. In particular, they disliked the French civil code, the lack of jury trials, and the absence of representative government.

Parliament, attempting to conciliate the loyalists and other British settlers, passed the far-reaching Constitutional, or Canada, Act in 1791. The Act, though it was the first statutory grant of limited self-government awarded to a British colony, earned fame mainly for its faults.

It created two provinces out of one—dividing Quebec into Upper Canada and Lower Canada, the former to be largely English-speaking and the latter chiefly French-speaking. The governments for these two colonies and for Nova Scotia were to be headed by Crown-appointed governors. The governors were to be advised by appointed legislative councils and elected assemblies. The assemblies themselves were granted limited powers and the franchise was restricted to property owners. The Act also designated Protestantism as the official religion, but did guarantee the right of worship to Roman Catholics.

As should have been easily foreseen, the creation of Upper and Lower Canada, along with the designation of Protestantism as the official religion, widened rather than closed the gap between the two cultures. And the council-assembly system (which was to be followed repeatedly throughout the course of Empire) put the limited self-rule in the hands of the wealthy. In each of the two new provinces, it reared a small elite that took control not only of local government but often of local commercial and fiscal institutions as well. In Upper Canada, the power group was the Family Compact, which thought nothing of the province's rural population. In Lower Canada, the Château Clique ruled, leaving the French trapper and farmer with little or no say in governmental matters. The rift and the discord created by the Act were to fester through the years and eventually break into open rebellion.

Other, more satisfactory changes, took place on the Canadian scene as the old century gave way to the new. While fur remained the principal source of revenue, newly arrived settlers discovered that wheat grew well in the northern climate. The crop that would one day rule Canadian agriculture—with an annual harvest topping the 23 million-bushel-mark by the 1970s—increased steadily as new farms were laid out deeper and deeper into the western plains region.

In addition, Bonaparte's rise to power and Europe's Napoleonic Wars of 1803–1815 brought added prosperity to Canada and the chance to cash in on yet another giant resource: its timber. When Napoleon cut off the Baltic ports where Britain had been buying wood, Canada's vast forests of pine and fir brought her an economic bonanza. She began shipping timber across the Atlantic in ever increasing quantities.

Other advantages resulted from the Napoleonic struggle. For a time, self-imposed restrictions on British trade idled the United States merchant marine. Shippers of a wide vari-

ety of commodities out of Halifax and St. Lawrence ports quickly grabbed up a commerce they had long coveted. In Britain, appreciation of the Canadian colonies as a storehouse of valued raw materials soared to new heights.

The War of 1812 saw American armies march once again on Canada. The invaders made some gains, but, with the defeat of Napoleon, Britain was able to dispatch a strong force to Canada, push out the Americans, and extend the colonial borders southward. The Treaty of Ghent, however, restored the border to its former position. Fur traders who had hungered for the return of pre-Revolutionary territory saw their hopes dashed.

Trappers were moving farther and farther west as the nineteenth century developed, but settlements were spreading westward, too, and farming and fur trapping were not compatible economic companions. The Hudson's Bay Company and the North West Company, the two giant trapping and trading firms of the day, competed for territory. On the Red River, in what was to become Manitoba, North West Company men massacred twenty-two members of a Hudson's Bay Company settlement. Court action and investigations followed, with the result that the two companies were merged under the Hudson's Bay banner in 1821. The single company held, by Crown charter, a huge tract stretching from Upper Canada and the shores of Hudson Bay to the Pacific and from the 49th parallel northward to the Arctic. It was called Rupert's Land, and company directors ruled it as a commercial autonomy. Theirs was a rule far less troublesome and complex than colonial administration.

As for colonial administration, the virtually powerless as-

semblies in Upper and Lower Canada were completely out
of patience with the ruling oligarchies by the 1830s. Joseph
Howe, a newspaper publisher and member of the assembly
in Nova Scotia, spoke out harshly against the governor and
the appointed council. Lower Canada's Louis J. Papineau
and Upper Canada's William Lyon Mackenzie, both leaders
in their respective assemblies, talked openly of rebellion.
They urged administrative changes and a constitution modeled after that of the United States. Priests, remembering the
French Revolution and the Roman Catholic Church's losses
at the time, tried to hold the French-speaking colonists in
check in the face of such oratorical outbursts. But to no avail.
In 1837, rebellion broke out in both provinces.

The outbreak barely rose above the level of armed rioting.
Redcoats brought the fighting to a halt within hours, with
the leaders then being carted off to prison. The uprising did
not win widespread support because, advocating an Ameri-
can-like constitution and having connections with certain
American patriots, it smacked of an unsavory foreign flavor
to even the most radical of Canadians. Whatever sympathy
it did have was lost in 1838 when volunteer armies from the
border states attempted to invade and "free" Canada.

Though the border incursions were turned back and peace
was soon restored, the rebellion greatly alarmed Parliament.
The lesson of the thirteen colonies was still remembered with
humiliation. Now, all steps must be taken—including a
measure of increased self-rule and even the amalgamation
of the Canadian colonies—to prevent the loss of the northern
possessions. Parliament decided to send one of its most out-
spoken members westward to investigate the situation and

make recommendations for its improvement. The decision stands as one of the most significant made by Parliament in the history of the Second Empire.

Named to the job was John George Lambton, First Earl of Durham, known to his wealthy Whig intimates as "Radical Jack" because of his democratic persuasions. He arrived in Quebec in May of 1838, armed with a commission from young Queen Victoria to investigate and report. To simplify his task and to give him the muscle necessary to see it through, he had been appointed governor-general of Canada.

Durham landed in the West with the preconceived notion that all the colonies should be united, but the cultural differences among the people and the country's vast geographic separations soon convinced him that immediate federation was not feasible. He did, however, recommend that Upper and Lower Canada be joined. Parliament agreed and united them into a single unit, calling it the province of Canada.

Neither Durham nor the Canadians considered the Upper-Lower Canada unification his most significant recommendation. What he said was most needed was precisely the cure that moderate colonial assemblies had long been urging: a parliamentary form of government, complete with a body of cabinet ministers, an elected body that would advise the colonial governors. Taking a healthy slap at the oligarchies that had long ruled Upper and Lower Canada with little regard for the common people, he reasoned that, if the Crown "has to carry on the Government in unison with a representative body, it must consent to carry it on by means of those in whom that representative body has confidence." [6]

The concept of a parliament in a colony marked a consequential departure from the old ideas of how an empire should be run. It was a concept befitting a man whose nickname was Radical Jack; it was one thing to have colonial assemblies asking for a parliament, but quite another to have the suggestion come from a representative of the homeland. Even more unusual was Durham's conviction, implicit in the recommendation, that a colony could govern all of its own affairs and still retain its ties with the mother country. His was a sophisticated view that called for a colonial policy far more liberal than the most generous offerings to date of partial self-rule. It called for a reasonable trust on the part of the mother country, an appreciation of the idea of loyalty on the part of the colony, and an understanding on the parts of both of the social, economic, and military advantages to be had in the association. It was to play an increasingly significant role in Britain's dealings with the more advanced of her holdings as the years went by and would be among the factors helping the Empire make its twentieth-century transition to the Commonwealth of Nations.

Durham's report today is looked upon as the Magna Carta of the British Empire. It proved too radical for his Parliament, however, and so it was shelved, but only for the time being. The ideas behind it had been planted. They would soon take root and bloom in Canada.

Though Durham's report was temporarily shelved, other factors were urging Britain to a new approach to empire. She had become an industrial nation through the years and now had an army of restive homeland manufacturers and merchants on her hands. They had goods to sell to the world,

and they were loudly objecting to the tariffs that Britain had long imposed on European imports competitive with merchandise being shipped in from the colonies. The European nations had retaliated with tariffs of their own. The lords of English commerce now wanted all trade restrictions ended so that they could cash in on a greater European import-export flow. Their demands were heard and, one by one, the homeland tariffs were abandoned throughout the early 1840s.

The canceling of the tariffs, which had been so protective of colonial interests, roused a question that finally led to Durham's report being taken off the shelf. If the colonies were to be cut free economically, then was it not only simple justice to give them political freedom as well? The British answer came in 1847 when, just seven years after it had been drafted, Durham's proposal for a Canadian parliament became law. Voters in Nova Scotia and Canada elected reform parties to office. Governors in both provinces told party leaders to form their governments and assume responsibility for internal affairs.

Adjustment to the new system posed many difficulties, particularly for members of the old oligarchies. But the overriding headache was economic. The dropping of the colonial tariffs meant that wheat growers, lumbermen, trappers, and fishermen had to go in search of new foreign markets, never an easy task in a competitive world. Finally, in 1854, in addition to contracts being developed with other nations, reciprocal trade agreements were established with the United States. Now fiscal and political independence could grow together.

When Durham had first come west, he had envisioned the unification of all Canada. His ideas of federation had been ahead of their time, but the constant growth taking place in the country was bringing them steadily to the point of possibility. What were to be known as the Maritime Provinces—Nova Scotia, New Brunswick, and Prince Edward Island—were taking shape in the eastern region that the French had called Acadia. Railroads were being constructed and, by the 1850s, they were linking the towns along the St. Lawrence with ice-free ports to the south; no longer need Quebec and Montreal fall into winter isolation. And, about the same time, the Hudson's Bay Company was talking of ceding British Columbia to the homeland government.

The award of the vast western tract came in 1858, followed closely by its designation as a Crown colony. Five years later, gold was discovered there along the Stikine River. The miners who rushed to the strike—they were mostly Americans—stayed on to settle the region.

These were but a few of the developments that hastened federation. The first formal step in that direction was taken in 1864 by the Maritime Provinces when delegates from Nova Scotia, New Brunswick, and Prince Edward Island met at Prince Edward's Charlottetown to discuss union. The province of Canada, with its government presently in a turmoil because of bickering between its French and English factions, was not invited to attend, but asked to be permitted to do so. As matters turned out, the delegates from Canada dominated the meeting, and a second session was convened at Quebec a few months later. Within two years, a third conference sat at London.

There were, of course, objections as the thrust toward federation took shape. Delegates from Prince Edward Island, seeing the proposal grow far beyond the simple alliance they had first imagined, withdrew. But the other delegates eventually agreed to a final plan and, in 1867, Parliament passed the British North American Act, creating the Dominion of Canada. United under its banner were four provinces—Ontario and Quebec (formerly the Upper and Lower Canadas), Nova Scotia, and New Brunswick—with their seat of government to be in Ottawa.

But there was a problem. The amalgamation was complete, but the four newborn provinces embraced little more than one-third of the vast British North American continent. Out to the west, the inviting British Columbia was separated from the federation by more than a thousand miles of Rupert's Land, the sprawling tract owned by the Hudson's Bay Company. British Columbia was too far removed to be brought easily into the federation, and the company acreage in between promised to make westward expansion of the federation difficult. The barrier was removed, however, in 1869. Because the age of the beaver was long past, the Hudson's Bay Company sold Rupert's Land to the government for three hundred thousand pounds, asking—and being granted—the right to reserve certain of its areas for hunting and fishing.

With the barrier gone, western expansion proceeded quickly. Manitoba joined the Dominion in 1870, followed by British Columbia a year later. Then, with the completion of the Canadian Pacific Railroad in the 1880s, settlers poured in from Ireland, Scotland, England, China, Japan, and other too-crowded nations, all attracted by the lure of free land.

They settled in British Columbia and Manitoba and in the intervening regions that, in 1905, would become the provinces of Saskatchewan and Alberta. Many built farms and enthroned wheat as the agricultural king of the west.

But there were other attractions. In the 1890s, gold strikes along the Klondike River drew thirty thousand miners to Yukon Territory in Canada's remote Northwest. When the gold gave out, just a few miners remained behind to work the land, but the strikes had taught Canadians that there was great wealth beneath their soil. In addition to her lumber and fishing industries, British Columbia would eventually produce silver, copper, gold, iron, lead, and zinc. Alberta would one day boast that she held 50 percent of Canada's coal reserves and drilled up 90 percent of the nation's oil. Saskatchewan was not only to harvest copper, zinc, gold, coal, and natural gas, but was destined to become the country's largest supplier of uranium. Though agriculture would continue to dominate Manitoba's economy, she, too, would produce copper, zinc, gold, silver, and cadmium, but all in limited quantities.

The West proved indeed a rich frontier for the Dominion. But the natural wealth did not end there. Lying above the western and central provinces, from British Columbia on the Pacific to Manitoba on Hudson Bay, are Canada's wilderness holdings—the Yukon Territory, the District of Mackenzie, the District of Keewatin, and the District of Franklin, the last stretching up through a clutter of Eskimo-inhabited islands to the Arctic Ocean. Sparsely settled and with much exploration of their natural resources yet to be done, these holdings promise to be a treasure house of mineral wealth. Gold has long been mined in the District of

Mackenzie, as it has along with silver, lead, and zinc in the Yukon. Surveys of oil and natural gas possibilities throughout these vast lands are presently under way. And, far to the east, a deposit of iron ore has been found in Newfoundland that may prove to be the richest in the world.

The late nineteenth century and the mid-twentieth century saw the final rounding out of Canada's borders. Prince Edward Island, whose delegates had withdrawn from the London federation talks, joined the Dominion in 1873 and became its smallest province. Newfoundland won dominion status for herself early in this century and then, with her long stretch of adjoining Labrador coast, linked with Canada as a province in 1949. With the completion of her borders, Canada became the second largest country in the world in area, exceeded only by the Soviet Union.

Despite the happy beginnings of western expansion, the development of a modern, prosperous Canada did not come easily. In the twentieth century, two world wars; dust-bowl conditions that struck certain agricultural areas because of prolonged dry weather and the over-planting of crops; and a world-wide economic depression that reached out to touch her combined to slow growth and hinder prosperity. Furthermore, the cultural clash between her French and English factions continued to be a problem, as it is today. But, regardless of these problems, this century has seen Canada reach maturity and, upon the transition from Empire to Commonwealth, join the new family of nations as an equal partner, while maintaining her traditional loyalties to the mother country.

As an independent nation, she has joined the United States as a partner in North American continental defense. Though she has sometimes been forced reluctantly into the polemics of the Cold War, she has proven a staunch ally. Her most significant role in this century, however, has been that of peacemaker.

In the Middle East crisis of 1956, Canada diverted England and France from an Egyptian war by submitting a compromise proposal to the United Nations General Assembly, which led to the establishment of an international force to keep the peace. That year, Canadian Prime Minister L. B. Pearson was awarded the Nobel Prize for Peace. Six years later, Pearson met with United States President Lyndon B. Johnson to urge settlement of the war in Vietnam. The plea for peace, endorsed by Canadian citizens, contributed materially to the start of the Paris peace talks.

Perhaps most symbolic of Canada's role as an independent, responsible nation was the Universal and International Exposition which was held at Montreal in 1967. Known more commonly as "Expo 67," the event marked the one-hundredth anniversary of Canadian federation and attracted to it exhibits from more than seventy nations. The theme of the exhibition—"Man and his World"—could not have been more fitting for a nation that, in the course of a century, had welcomed settlers from all over the globe to its lands, had developed from a collection of four provinces to a giant amalgamation of nine, and had emerged as one of the foremost international powers for peace.

Chapter Six

The Lion in the Pacific

WHILE MAORI CONFLICTS and British indifference delayed
the development of New Zealand, an attitude of caution—
dictated by the very nature of a penal colony—long restricted
progress in Australia. The early governors of the New South
Wales colony looked upon discovery, expansion, development, and, for that matter, any change whatsoever as a threat
to their administration and control of the prisoners. Official
policy restricted settlement to the Sydney and Hobart areas.

Matthew Flinders, the English naval captain who completed a charting of the entire Australian coast in 1803,
urged inland expeditions to fill in the map that he had out-
lined, but ten years passed before the first settlers crossed
the Blue Mountains and commenced the exploration of the
upper tributaries of the Murray River. Not until 1862, forty-
eight years after Flinders's death, did John McDouall Stuart

lead the first overland party across the length of the continent.

By then, however, the attitude of the Australian government toward development and expansion had changed drastically, with fervor replacing reluctance. What had brought about the change? In a single word: wool.

It was in this commodity that the island continent, whose endless miles of virgin territory would one day support a wide variety of farming and grazing enterprises, found one of its greatest resources. By the early twentieth century, Australia was housing some 100 million of the world's estimated 600 million sheep. Today, in a good year, its sheep generally surpass the 150 million mark, with about three-quarters of their number being Merinos, which are renowned for their high-quality wool, while the remainder are crossbreeds that are reared for meat and wool. In all, Australia accounts for more than a quarter of the world's annual wool production—about 1,000 million pounds a year.

Without doubt, wool was chiefly responsible for opening up the Australian interior to the white man. Its story begins with Captain John Macarthur, one of the most infamous members of the early Rum Corps, an adventurer who once boasted that he had engineered the dismissal of every colonial governor up to 1809. Though little national pride can be taken in his Australian beginnings, he is remembered today as the man who first brought sheep into the country. And while other coastal farmers soon were grazing herds of their own and contributing to New South Wales's agrarian self-sufficiency, it was Macarthur who took the lead in promoting wool as a commodity for export.

For many years, the English textile industry ignored the samples of long, silky wool that Macarthur sent from the far side of the globe, but in 1822, with domestic sheepmen facing ruin from imports of inexpensive but high-grade German wool, the samples from Australia suddenly loomed as a salvation, particularly when manufacturers took a second look at their quality and then learned that their fibers mixed well with those produced at home. The lords of English commerce now saw the distant island continent in a new light. It held great possibilities. It could be something more than a dumping ground for unwanted humanity. Investment there might reap a handsome profit.

Grazing companies began to take shape, applying to the Crown for New South Wales land grants. Among the first in line was the Australian Agricultural Company, which received six hundred thousand acres and sent Sir Edward Parry, the famous Arctic explorer, out to manage the holding. The company's success, though not achieved without difficulty, encouraged other investors and the award of further land grants. Soon it was necessary to look beyond New South Wales for acreage.

The opening of hitherto unsettled Australian territory was under way.

The Western Australia Company received a grant of one million acres and under the leadership of its chief investor, Thomas Peel, set out in 1829 to establish a settlement at the mouth of the Swan River on the continent's southwest coast. With James Stirling, who had been appointed lieutenant-governor for the settlement, he led eight hundred men and women to an unsurveyed and unfriendly land, where he was

immediately beset by misfortune. Fencing for the sheep had
to await the completion of surveys and, as a consequence,
much of the livestock wandered away to starve, to die from
eating a poisonous weed, or to end up on the cooking fires
of the Aborigines. Then a labor shortage sent wages soaring.
Discouraged settlers fled the region by the boatload, leaving
Peel and Stirling with but a handful of pioneers. Eventually, though, the company managed to talk Parliament into
sending out convict labor, and the venture, with an assist
from a successful wheat crop, at last managed to get on its
feet. Incidentally, the transportation of convicts to the south-
west area continued until 1868, long after public outcries had
put an end to the practice in the rest of Australia. Today,
Perth and Freemantle stand on the sites of the company's
early settlements, the biggest cities in Australia's biggest
state.

A growing demand for land, combined with the early
failure of the Swan River venture, prompted the birth of
yet another settlement—this time, an illegal one. Port Phillip
on the southeastern coast had been off limits by colonial
policy since 1803, for, even though there was excellent farming and grazing land thereabouts, governors feared loss of
control if settlements were permitted. But land-hungry farmers from Tasmania and refugees from the Swan River project ignored the ban. It was not the first time, nor would it
be the last, that men took unauthorized possession of Crown
lands. Squatters, as we shall see, were to complicate Australian land tenures for many decades to come. Nothing was
done, however, to stop the Port Phillip settlement. In time,
it became the city of Melbourne, and the region around it
the state of Victoria.

In 1831, Parliament, reacting to the growing demand for sheep land and now beginning to see Australia as a valuable possession whose future welfare could best be served by an orderly rather than a come-and-get-it development, abolished free land grants. Backing Parliament to the hilt in its decision was Edward Gibbon Wakefield, whose interest in prisons and penal colonies stemmed from his own three-year jail sentence for eloping with an heiress against her parents' wishes. If investors had to pay for the land, he argued, Australia would attract men with the means and the sense of responsibility to improve their holdings to the utmost. The revenues, he added, should be used to pay the passage for young married couples from crowded England to the population-starved continent "down under." Wakefield wanted to test his theories on the south-central coast, and in 1839 Parliament gave him his chance by passing an act that created the South Australian Company. His first settlement of land-buying pioneers was put down at the mouth of the Murray River, years later developing into the city of Adelaide, the capital of today's state of South Australia.

In a later year, Wakefield led a band of colonists to New Zealand, there establishing the cities of Wellington on North Island and Nelson on South Island. He named the former in honor of his friend, the Duke of Wellington, long a supporter of his Australian ideas, and the latter for the British naval hero, Lord Horatio Nelson, who earlier in the century had lost his life at the Battle of Trafalgar.

Sheep-raising was not all that was on Australia's mind in the beginning 1800s. The island continent was also the scene of much political change, especially in the New South Wales area, which, despite growing settlements elsewhere, continued to hold the franchise on wealth and population. It was change that one day would result in self-government for Australia.

It began in 1823 and was continued in 1825 and 1828 with a series of modest changes that Parliament enacted for the New South Wales government. Known collectively as the Reform Acts, they created appointed executive and legislative councils to advise the governor, established a colonial supreme court, and provided for jury trials. Parliament called for their enactment because Australia's growing wealth and attraction for free settlers made it increasingly apparent that New South Wales could not long remain a penal colony. Steps had to be taken to open the way to a style of government more befitting a conventional colony.

One facet of the Reform Acts caused a brief but conseqential battle in Sydney. As was pointed out in the earlier Australian chapter, the New South Wales population of the early 1800s was divided into two opposing camps—the emancipists and the exclusionists, the former consisting of men who had first come to Australia as prisoners and then had won their freedom, and the latter of settlers who had arrived as free men and who insisted that they alone had the right to own land and hold public office. At the time of the Acts, the governor, Sir Ralph Darling, was a firm pro-exclusionist, and he made certain that no emancipist's name was included in the first jury lists. William Charles Wentworth, an attorney-newspaper publisher, the first Australian ever to be admitted to the English bar, launched a scathing attack on the governor in his *The Australian*. Darling tried to suppress the publication, but the newly established supreme court blocked his every effort. He sued Wentworth for libel, only to have the publisher counter with impeachment proceedings that finally brought about his recall. The incident saw the emancipists win their first formal measure of equality in the new country.

The next change came in 1840 when Parliament ordered that the transportation of prisoners to New South Wales be stopped. The step was taken after a parliamentary committee charged with studying the practice reported that it was costing Britain about half a million pounds a year.

Coincidentally, no sooner had Parliament halted the New South Wales transportation than a four-year depression hit Australia's wool-based economy. There had been too much speculation and too much development on credit during the previous decade. Thus in 1840, when an over-supply of wool sent prices crashing on the world market, one Australian venture after another collapsed. Banks closed. Sheep were slaughtered for their tallow in a feeble attempt to cover losses. Sheepmen abandoned the land and moved to the towns to beg for work. Some starved in the streets. When the "bad times," as they were called, finally passed, the industry slowly got back to its feet, but sheepmen were now wiser and investors more cautious in their financial dealings. The new attitude provided a sounder foundation for Australia's economic future.

Though the transportation of prisoners continued to Tasmania until 1853 and to Western Australia until 1868, its end in New South Wales opened the way for the first real step toward self-government. Responding to pleas from the

colony, Parliament in 1842 granted it a legislative council
of twenty-four elected members to serve with twelve appointed by the governor. The council's assignment was to
advise the governor on most domestic affairs. Tainted with
some leftover exclusionist prejudices—not to mention a few
British aristocratic snobberies—it was hardly a democratic
body. A man had to hold ten thousand dollars' worth of
property before he could sit on the council, and a voter had
to own one thousand dollars' worth before he could go to
the polls to vote for a councilman. But, despite its flaws, it
gave the colony its first voice in its own destiny.

The major political issue of the day was land ownership.
Squatters were everywhere and, because of the property requirement for office, they dominated the council. Sir George
Gipps, who served as governor from 1838 to 1846 and who is
ranked as one of the colony's ablest administrators, found
himself at constant odds with them. He wanted to preserve
the land for future development and, in an attempt to put
the brakes on their helter-skelter spread, he enforced an
existing but much-ignored regulation which required them
to buy a renewable license for the privilege of holding and
working their properties. The squatters, of course, resisted
the idea, for it obviously implied that their tenure depended
on the license and that their rights to the land would expire
with the periodic expiration of the license. Gipps won the
licensing battle, but he had little success with other land
reforms.

For example, shocked to find that one man held twenty-
seven sheep stations under one license and that all of the
great Liverpool Plain was in the hands of just eight men,

Gipps tried to win approval for regulations that would allow a squatter to buy part of his property and leave the remainder available for purchase by other settlers. The squatters replied by threatening to cut off wool exports. English textile interests, foreseeing disaster, successfully put pressure on Parliament for Gipps's removal, and he became one more victim of colonial in-fighting. A year after his departure from office, he died of a heart disease brought on by his struggles.

Despite the unending battle over property ownership, Parliament decided that the legislative council was setting a good pattern for the future of Australia and extended it to Western Australia and South Australia in 1850. In the same year, Victoria became a separate colony with a legislative council of its own. When Tasmania departed from the mainland government in 1855, it began its own operation with the New South Wales council system. Queensland followed suit in 1859.

While the spread of self-rule was a significant political trend during the 1850s, an event occurred at the start of the decade that was to change the course of Australian history even further. In February 1851, a farmer named Edward Hargreaves came into Sydney with a pouch full of gold nuggets that he had found near his home on the Bathurst Plains west of the Great Dividing Range. Gold had been found earlier in the area, but conservative governors, fearing that a gold rush would undermine their control, had always managed to suppress any news of the finds.

But not this time. Australia was in need of newcomers, for much of the population had packed off to California in the three years since gold had been discovered there. And so the news of the Bathurst find was announced to the world. The result: a rush to Australia that rivaled the one to California and, at century's end, to Alaska.

Men flocked to Sydney from Europe and America, marching inland from there with pick, shovel, and gold pan. They came first in the hundreds and then in the thousands as the word of one rich strike after another found its way to the outside world. Sydney basked in an unprecedented business boom, with its merchants, saloon keepers, and hotel managers becoming wealthy overnight.

Leaders of the newly formed Victoria colony to the south looked on with envy. Businessmen in the colony's principal city, Melbourne, decided to do something about the situation. They saw no reason why Sydney should get all the trade, and so they offered a reward to any prospector who found gold within two hundred miles of their city.

Remarkably, within weeks, men were swaggering or reeling drunkenly down the main street to claim the reward. They had made strikes at Golden Gully, Bendigo, and Ballarat that were to prove far richer than any made in New South Wales. The human tide flowed down into Victoria.

While gold production from the Victoria fields declined gradually over the years—from $81,500,000 in 1852 to $39,-000,000 in 1861—the number of miners grew steadily during the decade. They were a crew not easily governed. Many had come for adventure and a quick fortune. Many simply wanted to escape the authoritarian rules of their European homelands. Most held liberal views, and not a few were members of the Chartist movement, which advocated the rights of the laboring man and called for universal male suffrage. Thanks to a tragedy that befell the Chartists and their fellow miners at the Ballarat diggings in 1854, the right of the ballot was finally given to every Australian male, whether he owned property or not.

The tragedy was a result of the Victoria government's effort to regulate the untidy flood of newcomers by demanding that all miners buy a monthly license for the privilege of digging; any prospector caught without one and with a busy shovel in hand was promptly tossed into jail. If a man had a rich vein on his hands, the cost of the license was of no consequence, but, when the diggings were thin, the fee could prove impossible. Many gold seekers tried to work without a license, but the local police—some of whom had started life "down under" as Tasmanian convicts—took a delight in hunting them down, all too often beating and harassing them before locking them in a cell. The miners at Ballarat finally rebelled against the practice, burned their licenses, and united under a twenty-seven-year-old Irishman named Peter Lalor to protect their rights. The government retaliated by sending 450 soldiers to the mines. The miners, intending to make a stand, constructed a stockade on Eureka flat under Lalor's direction. But the attack came early in the morning when most of the defenders were asleep. The soldiers killed thirty miners, some still in their blankets, and stood several others up to be shot after they had surrendered.

News of the slaughter outraged the citizens of Melbourne. The government hastened to pass political reforms. The monthly mining license requirement was dropped. Amend-

ments were made in the colonial constitution. They not
only provided for universal male suffrage but also did away
with the property requirement for holding office. In 1856,
the Victorian legislative council adopted the famous secret
or "Australian ballot" for all elections. As for Lalor, he was
elected to the council and served for many years, including
six as Speaker.

The second half of the nineteenth century was marked
by arguments over the rights of squatters to the land they
held. Those rights had always depended on the make-up of
the colonial councils; so long as the councils had been
dominated by squatters, the rights had been secure, with
the members saying that the squatters actually owned the
property which they occupied. But, in the second half of
the century, thanks to the death of the property requirement for holding office, the councils broke free of squatter
domination; now the members claimed that the squatters
did not really own their land and had no right to it. In a
move to clear them out, the councils enacted legislation that
authorized the sale of squatter land to settlers and that con-
spired to keep the squatters from buying great chunks of it.
But the squatters hired agents or "dummies" to buy vast
portions as soon as the sale opened. Thus, a law that was
designed to loosen the grip of the squatters enabled them to
buy as much land as they wanted, purchases that were eventually deemed to be legal.

With the law, South Australia managed to develop a reasonable balance between farmland owned by settlers and
pasture land owned by squatters. It became known for its
fine vineyards, but, in New South Wales, squatter domina-

tions continued. An 1883 survey showed that eight million acres of pasture land was in the hands of just ninety-six persons.

The men who worked and managed the remote sheep stations led a lonely existence. In the small country town, the only link with civilization was provided by the stagecoach, much as it was in the western America of the day. Its arrival was always awaited with excitement and, if it were a Cobb and Company stage, the anticipation was justified. The firm was started by four Yankee gold-seekers who gave the company its name and who then, going into other businesses, sold it to another gold-seeker, James Rutherford. He ran the company with a flourish, importing crack drivers from America, roaming the countryside for the best horses, and purchasing custom-made rigs at three thousand dollars each. His methods and showmanship made all competing stage outfits seem pale by comparison, and soon Cobb and Company ruled the roads from Victoria to Queensland, hauling both passengers and freight.

It was always a pleasure to encounter a Cobb stage on the road, to watch the graceful lines of its team and rig swing over the horizon and stand fleetingly silhouetted against a cloudless sky. But it was no pleasure to encounter certain other traffic composed of brutal men who looted, robbed, and murdered to acquire wealth. Gangs of these outlaws—"bushrangers," the Australians called them—were to be found everywhere. They robbed stages, waylaid lone ranchers heading home with fresh supplies, and attacked sheep stations, driving off the stock and burning the outbuildings to the ground. One band—Ben Hall and his gang—once captured a whole town and held its citizens as hostages while staging footraces and downing drinks unwillingly provided by the local saloon.

Hall was felled by troopers in 1865 at the age of twenty-eight, but others of his ilk had long lives. For many years, Captain Thunderbolt "harvested" the traffic on what was known as the Main Northern Road above Sydney. Once, after separating the members of a touring German band from their money, he ordered them to line up and play a few tunes for him. The most famous of the bushrangers, however, was Ned Kelly whose domain ranged through the settlements on the New South Wales–Victoria border. Cool and audacious, the Kelly gang once took over a police station, locked up its officers, and used their uniforms to masquerade as visiting lawmen for a weekend. On Monday morning, they strode into the local bank and walked off with what one townsman called "a damn big withdrawal." Kelly and his men customarily wore armor pounded out of plowshares as protection against troopers' bullets, but the leader was finally dropped by a shot in the leg. He went to the gallows for his crimes.

Regarded by some Australians as Robin Hoods and romanticized by historians, the bushrangers were nonetheless a cruel and heartless lot, adding to the hardships and dangers of frontier Australia. But that they were an interesting phenomenon in the passing scene of the nation's nineteenth-century social life cannot be denied.

More deserving of romantic recollection were the huge grain ships that hauled the produce of the Western Australia and Victoria wheat fields to the flour mills of England. These tall square-riggers raced each other around Cape Horn, risking shipwreck or dismasting for the honor of being first to drop anchor at Freemantle or Melbourne. Once loaded, they would dash for home. If passage in either direction took more than one hundred days, their skippers considered it a poor showing. The sailing ships continued in service well into the age of steam, but, by the 1920s, rising labor costs and cheap Diesel power drove them from the seas, marking the end of the great era of sail.

Once recovered from the "bad times" of the 1840s, Australia's economy grew with vigor. Of importance from the earlier penal colony days, farming caught up with grazing to enrich the country, with both wheat and wool production increasing steadily each year. Sugar-cane plantations sprang up in tropical Queensland. Then came new mineral discoveries. In addition to the gold unearthed in New South Wales, Victoria, and later Western Australia (discovered there in 1893), iron ore was dug in South Australia. In the years up to and into the twentieth century copper and zinc were found in Tasmania; copper, tin, silver, lead, and zinc in Queensland and New South Wales; brown coal in Victoria; and bituminous coal in New South Wales. As mining operations grew, so did factories. By the start of this century, most cities had industries producing goods for both foreign and domestic consumption.

The 1880s were by far the country's most bountiful years. In 1883, workers completed a direct rail route between Sydney and Melbourne. Three years later, Victoria launched the first government irrigation project. Then, in 1887, the first cargo of frozen Australian lamb was delivered aboard

In 1893, New Zealand became the first country in the world to grant voting rights to women over twenty-one years of age. With the ballot in hand, women encouraged further reforms, including non-contributory old age benefits. The way was cleared during the decade for state ownership of public utilities and the government's control of prices and wages.

Thus the foundations were laid for a system of socialism that has grown with remarkable success through the years and that remains the New Zealand approach to government to this day.

In Australia, while the leaders of colonial government did not preoccupy themselves with reform politics, they had another issue much in mind: federation. The idea of joining the separate colonies under one central government had been discussed as early as 1860, but few of the independent, competitive men of the day had favored it, each preferring to see his region pursue its own fortune and destiny. New South Wales, the oldest and wealthiest of the colonies, was especially opposed to any suggestion that it surrender its role of leadership to a federal banner.

In the 1880s, however, Germany and France increased their holdings in the South Pacific, and the Australian colonies began mulling over the idea of mutual defense. Delegates from the various colonies met at Sydney in 1883 to discuss the matter and, as could be expected, the talk finally got around to federation. Out of the session came the Australian Federal Council, a body of colonial representatives charged with consideration of matters of mutual concern and with the promotion of a federal system. With no backing whatsoever from New South Wales, it was doomed from the start, but two events occurred in 1888 that kept the federation impulse alive. First, the legislatures of all colonies agreed to contribute to the construction of an Australian navy. Second, both Australia and New Zealand sent delegations to Melbourne for a further hashing out of the federation question.

New Zealand, because of its great distance from Australia in those days of sailing ships and because it held national aims of its own, was no more interested in federation than was New South Wales, but the other delegates ended up by agreeing to draft a federal constitution. Their decision launched a long series of meetings and debates that led to the 1891 Sydney Convention where a constitution modeled closely on that of the United States was written.

Citizens, however, did not get the chance to vote on the new document for six years, principally because of opposition from New South Wales. When a referendum was finally held, the voters of New South Wales were the only ones who did not give it the necessary majority for adoption. A second vote, held after the colony had been promised the capital city for the new federation (Canberra, which is located within the confines of New South Wales but which, in common with Washington, D.C., stands on federal land, has served as the nation's capital since 1927), elicited approval of the constitution, after which it went to Parliament in London for further debate.

There, it underwent lengthy consideration and some revision, but, due to the same liberal colonial tendencies that had won self-government for Canada some years earlier, it was finally authorized. On January 1, 1901, by royal proclamation, the Commonwealth of Australia came into being.

The federation consisted—as it does today—of the five mainland states of New South Wales, Queensland, Victoria, Western Australia, and South Australia, and the island of Tasmania. Also housed within the federation is the 520,280-square-mile block of sparsely populated (thirty-seven thousand people in the 1960s) land known as the Northern Territory. Originally a part of New South Wales, it belonged to South Australia in 1901, but passed to the federal government in 1911 and has remained under its jurisdiction ever since, functioning since 1947 with a legislative council.

Pursuing her own national destiny and remaining aloof from the newly created federation, New Zealand graduated from a colony to dominion status in 1907.

Both the nations "down under" entered the twentieth century as free and independent members of the British Empire. The new century would see them contribute wealth to the Empire and men to the British cause in World Wars I and II. Then, as the century witnessed the transformation of the Empire into the Commonwealth of Nations, with the attendant loss of certain British holdings, it would see them remain loyally with the mother country within the framework of the new amalgamation of states.

Chapter Seven

The Lion in the East

NEITHER THE PALATINATE WAR (1689–1697) nor the War of the Spanish Succession (1702–1713) reached out to touch India, and so the British East India Company and the French Compagnie de Indes Orientales managed to live peaceably alongside each other in their factories there until well into the eighteenth century, their desire for trade profits keeping a lid on any national antagonism that one might feel for the other But the third of the four great British–French engagements in Europe—the War of the Austrian Succession (1744–1748)—brought see-saw fighting to the Indian Ocean and ended for all time this tolerant competition. Throughout that war and the fifteen-year peace that followed it, the two companies fought an unending battle, each determined to undermine the prestige of the other.

The most critical aspect of their fighting centered on the

fold-up of the Mogul Empire and the return of India to its old network of independent kingdoms. Kings and princes scrambled for power in many of the re-emerging states and, in two of the peninsula's richest areas, the companies early in the War of the Austrian Succession backed opposing candidates for the native thrones, each hoping to see the other driven out should his men win. As for the candidates, they were eager for the help of the companies. Needed were their money, their sophisticated and deadly European-made weapons, the troops that they could muster, and the well-trained officers they could assign to lead Indian soldiers.

The areas involved were the Deccan, with its assortment of small states and, south toward the peninsular tip, the Carnatic region. Their thrones went up for grabs by relatives upon the deaths of their rulers in the 1740s. On behalf of their candidate in the Carnatic—and to further the cause of the War of the Austrian Succession—the French in 1746 attacked Madras—the East India Company's head-quarters on the east side of the peninsula—took it over, and held it until its return to the British at war's end in 1748. They then supported their candidates in the Deccan states by manning the Indian forces there with French officers. In the first years of the struggle, the Compagnie de Indes Orientales very definitely held the better cards.

But the high-stakes game was not destined to run indefinitely with the French. The hands began to turn against them with the arrival on the scene of a young East India office worker named Robert Clive.

Historians have used a variety of terms to describe this man around whom so much Indian history was to be played in the next years and who was to lay the foundations for British imperial rule there. They have called him adventurer, opportunist, scoundrel, economic brigand, great military and civil leader, plotter, and genius. All are legitimate descriptions of the man, but all can be superseded by one overall incapsulation of his character—restless and ruthless man of action. This indeed he was and, as such, he found in the now more turbulent than ever India the perfect stage on which to exercise his talents. If ever the right man came to the right country at the right time, it was Robert Clive. There, he transformed himself from an unruly youth into a historical figure of awesome proportions, doing so in less than two decades.

Born in 1725 in Shropshire, he came of one of the oldest and most respected families in England. As a boy, coltish, headstrong, and obstreperous, he promised to be little more than an embarrassment to the family and so, when he was eighteen years old, they got him out of sight by packing him off to Madras, where he began his career with the East India Company as a "writer," one of the countless young men who transcribed the company's purchase orders and its voluminous correspondence. His first years in India indicated nothing of the greatness to come, marked as they were by a duel with a fellow employee and an enduring moroseness that caused him twice to attempt suicide.

He began, however, to come into his own with the 1746 attack on Madras. When the factory fell to the French, he was taken prisoner but promptly escaped and made his way to nearby Fort St. David. His daring caught the eye of the governor there and he was given a military commission, that of ensign. The appointment set him up to take advantage of the critical events that occurred in 1751.

In that year, French and native troops put under siege the Carnatic fortress city of Trichinopoly. Housed within was Mohammed Ali, the East India Company's candidate for the region's throne. Clive talked his superiors into putting him at the head of a small force that would divert the attackers from Trichinopoly by capturing Arcot, the capital city of Chanda Sahib, the French-backed contestant in the Carnatic. At the head of three hundred natives and two hundred European soldiers, he marched on Arcot and captured it in early September. Then he settled his men down behind its barricades and successfully rode out a fifty-three day onslaught by Chanda's brother.

The daring and success of the campaign dealt a severe blow to French prestige, and the decline of the Compagnie's influence in India can be said to date from it. Clive further humiliated the French in a string of guerrilla skirmishes, after which, following a brief return to England, he was named governor of Fort St. David and promoted to the rank of lieutenant colonel. Then, in 1756, the series of events began to take shape through which he would bring the East India Company to the threshold of its greatest days in India.

The setting against which they were to be played out was Calcutta, the company's headquarters on the northern shores of the Bay of Bengal. Here, the surrounding area had been ruled by a succession of increasingly independent Mogul viceroys during the declining years of the Empire, the East India Company trading there with their consent. Now, the latest of their number, a young prince named

Siraj-ud-Daula, decided to be rid of the Britishers. His reasons were several, ranging from the fear the British intrusions in local affairs, now so prevalent elsewhere, might one day be directed against his realm, to anger over increased commercial advantages being sought by the company. He mounted an attack against the Calcutta factory in early June, easily capturing it and taking its occupants prisoner.

News of the fall of the trading post was bad enough, but it was accompanied by word of the terrible fate that had befallen 146 of the prisoners. Siraj-ud-Daula, so the story went, had ordered them—men, women, and children alike —herded into a guardroom to be kept there all through a sweltering night. The guardroom, which came to be known popularly as the Black Hole of Calcutta, measured only eighteen feet by fourteen feet ten inches. It had but two small windows, and in the morning only twenty-three of the prisoners remained alive, the rest having died of suffocation or heat prostration.

The story of the incident, luridly told in those days, has been pretty much discredited as gross exaggeration or sheer trickery. Author and journalist Joe David Brown observes that some historians are skeptical of the Black Hole and regard it as a hoax, an outrage invented by the English. He adds that, without doubt, many of its details are out-and-out fancy, among them the claim that some of the survivors, driven mad by thirst, sucked the perspiration from the clothes of their suffocated friends.[7]

If it was a hoax, the reason for its invention may be obvious. The East India Company, meddling in India's internal

affairs, consorting with potentates, and fattening itself on a
people that many back home pitied as being the naïve victims of western exploitation, was not regarded kindly in
many English quarters, and the company may well have
fabricated the whole story in an effort to win public sympathy, and an ensuing quiet, for its Indian enterprises. And,
if the tale was mere exaggeration, again the hand of the
company can be seen, or at least the imaginative excesses
of an eager press with a best-selling sensation on its hands.

No matter whether the accounts of the Black Hole were
fiction or exaggeration, the loss of the important Calcutta
factory demanded retaliation. And that is precisely what it
got. The company placed Clive and Admiral Charles Watson at the head of a three-thousand-man force and sent them
north out of Madras in early 1757. With Watson supporting
him from the sea, Clive re-took the post, faced the defeated
Siraj, and forced him to put on paper all the commercial
rights that his assault on the factory had violated. Added
were a string of new trading advantages that the company
had long sought.

The matter might have closed there had Siraj-ud-Daula
retired to his palace, licked his wounds, and behaved himself. But, humiliated, he had no intention of keeping his
agreement with the upstart Clive; and, a natural-born in-
triguer, he began plotting with the French for a fresh attempt at ousting the British. Clive, learning what was in
the wind, decided that the man had to be dethroned and
replaced with someone who would prove more pliable in
British hands. He marched his 3,000-man army, consisting
of 2,200 Indian and 800 European troops, against the prince's

forces, meeting them in the fields surrounding the village of Plassey, which lies near the city of Krishnagar north of Calcutta. Here, he defeated an army of fifty thousand men, broke the troublesome Siraj once and for all, and gave the East India Company beginning control of the Bengal area, a region that, fanning out west, north, and east of Calcutta, was one of India's richest dominions, as it is today.

That Clive's force, outnumbered at least sixteen to one, was able to defeat Siraj's army seems a military miracle. The miracle, however, reduces itself to more conventional proportions when a closer look is taken at the prince's troops, particularly his officer corps. Many of his officers were displeased with his rule and quite willing to see him overthrown. Others, including a general, were not above being bribed into conspiring against him. Long before the battle, they were meeting secretly with Clive and throwing their lot in with him. Plassey then, with Indian soldiers of the line functioning under treacherous orders, is recorded in history less as a military engagement than as a *coup d'état* at the close of a long period of intrigue.

With the fall of Bengal, the ultimate ascendancy of British power and trade over those of all other competitors in India became a foregone conclusion, and the pattern first of company, and then of London, involvement in and direction of Indian internal affairs was firmly set. Clive put Mir Jahar, a puppet ruler, on the throne and obtained for the company the privilege of collecting Bengalese taxes, a portion of which were to be given to the ruler, with the remainder—the lion's share—going to the company. This began a practice that would be later duplicated in other areas; it would disrupt the Indian economy and would rank high among the factors finally inducing London to take over the reins of India from the company. Clive also assumed control of Bengal's treasury and did not hesitate to dip into it to make rich men of himself and his lieutenants. That such behavior smacked of thievery seemed not to have crossed his mind or, if so, to have been immediately thrust aside. As a writer for the company, he had worked on a commission basis and now, since he had acquired a vast tract for his employers and had netted them a bonanza in taxes, he felt it only just to take a sizable profit for himself. He summed up his view of that profit with a dry and succinct: "I stand astonished at my own moderation." [8]

In gratitude for his conquest, the company appointed him governor of Bengal, a position that he held from 1757 to 1760 and from 1765 to 1767. During his first term, he strengthened the company's hold on Bengal, and, during his second, he extended it to an adjoining state. Two years before he took office, the French and Indian War had broken out in the Americas. By the time he ended his first tour of duty, the conflict had spread to Europe to become the Seven Years War.

The dislodgement of the French that had begun with Clive's daring and successful attack on Arcot in 1751 was completed in the Seven Years War. In 1763, the Treaty of Paris, along with depriving France of Canada, reduced her Indian holdings to Pondicherry near the peninsular tip and a handful of other trading posts, most of them commercially insignificant.

With Bengal, the East India Company embarked on a

program of expansion that was to continue through the first four decades of the nineteenth century and that was to succeed admirably in the teeth of repeated efforts to grind it to a halt.

As a start, the ruler of Oudh, Bengal's neighboring state, surged across the border with an army in 1764 in an effort to oust the company. He met with disaster at the battle of Buxor, after which Clive, just starting his second governorship, turned Oudh into a buffer state to protect the company's interests from further assaults from the interior. Other nearby areas were made into buffer states in later years. Oudh escaped the British hold for a time, but returned early in the nineteenth century.

Next, the company had to deal with the independent state of Mysore, which embraced a huge tract in the southwest of the peninsula. Its ruler challenged the spreading British authority, and General Cornwallis, making up for his humiliating loss at Yorktown, marched on the state in the early 1790s and secured half of it for the company. At century's end, after a period of uneasy peace, Mysore's remaining half was gained in a treaty signed at the close of bloody fighting in which its ruler was killed.

Finally, there was the Maratha Empire. It was a loose confederation of semi-independent states which had sprung up during the decline of the Mogul Empire to spread from west to east across central India. Its various states were determined to halt the company, thanks in part to some high-handed dealings with them by East India officials at Bombay. They were aided by French army officers who came in to train native troops during Napoleon's reign and who

hoped that a Maratha win over the company might herald
the rebirth of French power in India. But, in a series of
wars, a series of treaties, a series of alliances, and a series of
out-and-out briberies, the company managed to secure Maratha territory from both east and west between the late
eighteenth century and 1820. By that year, the bulk of central India was in British hands.

Finally, in three wars, fought in 1843, 1845–46, and 1848,
the British extended their influence up through the northern
and northwestern areas, the location of the two giant states
of Punjab and Sind.

The seeds for these final annexations were planted in the
1830s, in Afghanistan, India's neighbor to the northwest.
There, Shah Shuja, a ruler on good terms with the British,
was overthrown, and the news came down to India that his
successor was making friendly overtures to Russia, whose
influence presently extended into Persia. The British, fearful
that a Russian entry into Afghanistan might be the prelude
to an advance on India, immediately dispatched a force up
through the Sind to restore Shah Shuja to his throne, an
assignment that was successfully completed in short order.
But the force was soon beset by a general uprising of Afghanistan tribes, for the Shah was far from popular with
his people. The British pulled back to India in one of the
most disastrous retreats in military history. The tribes pursued and attacked on all sides. Out of a Redcoat army of
four thousand men and twelve thousand camp followers,
only one British officer and a few Indians reached safety.

The debacle filled the Punjab and Sind states with con-
tempt for the hated white man who had subjugated so much

of their India. Further, the British had violated a treaty of several years standing with Sind by using it as a base for the Afghan invasion, and in 1843 the Sind ruler stormed the headquarters of the state's British liaison officer. The British retaliated with attacks that brought Sind to its knees and forced it to submit to full British control.

The adjoining state of Punjab now feared that the British, flushed with the Sind success, might look greedily in its direction. To forestall such a possibility, Punjab struck first, sending an army across the border and into British territory. The native troops were soundly defeated in a series of battles, with Punjab then being placed under British administration. But the Punjabs refused to sit quietly by and rose up in arms in 1848. Their army was destroyed in the battle of Hujarat, after which the state was locked firmly in British grasp.

The extension of the East India Company was at an end.

In the closing years of the eighteenth century and the first four decades of the nineteenth British power extended farther than India. Significant territorial acquisitions were made elsewhere in the Indian Ocean, among the Indonesian islands at the edge of the Pacific, and up the eastern face of Asia at Hong Kong.

The first acquisitions were Ceylon and a small dot of land on the Cape of Good Hope. The former, a 25,332-square-mile island off the southeastern tip of India, had been early occupied by the Portuguese in their push into the Indian Ocean, but had been lost to the Dutch in the latter half of the seventeenth century. During the same period, the Dutch had planted a little colony on the Cape, giving themselves a servicing point for their eastbound ships. Because of a European war that broke out in 1792, both were destined to fall into British hands.

In that year, on the eve of Napoleon's ascendancy, France, torn with internal strife, was at war again, this time with Austria and Prussia. It was a struggle in which she was soon also fighting with Britain and Holland. When France overran Holland and forced her to change sides, Britain in 1795 landed troops at Ceylon, at the Cape colony, and at Sumatra and Java in the Indonesians, taking them over and planning to hold them "in trust" for the deposed and pro-British Dutch ruler.

Napoleon came to power during the war and the struggle merged into the Napoleonic campaigns, which did not end until his final defeat in 1815. In the international agreements that followed the Bonaparte collapse, Britain returned Java and Sumatra to the Dutch, but maintained her hold on Ceylon and the Cape colony, along with the Indian Ocean island of Mauritius, which she had captured from the French. With her South Atlantic holdings—the tiny Ascension Island and the larger St. Helena, which had been taken from the Dutch in 1673 and which now housed the exiled Napoleon—they formed a chain of convenient servicing stations for East India Company shipping, not to mention a chain of well-placed military bases should there be further wars in the Indian Ocean.

The desire to protect her route to China, an old market on the Pacific, brought England her next acquisition. In the seventeenth century, the East India Company had managed to establish a trading post at Canton, from which tea and silk were transported to India aboard what the company called "country ships," there to be transferred to larger vessels for the run to England. Though China was indifferent to outside commerce and disdained foreigners, the Canton post had thrived and, in the early nineteenth century, was responsible for a lively and profitable trade.

But there were some problems on the horizon. An increasing number of nations were looking at China with a commercial gleam in their eyes. And the Dutch, always a threat to any East India ship that nosed into the Pacific, were back in the Indonesians now that the war in Europe was over.

At least one Englishman thought that Britain should take steps to protect its India-China route. He thought it a pity, too, that London had handed Java and Sumatra back to the Dutch at the close of the Napoleonic campaigns. While in residence there, Britain had gotten a commercial foothold in the Pacific. It really shouldn't be given up. Rather, it should be expanded. He was Sir Stamford Raffles, who had served as lieutenant governor of Sumatra during the British Indonesian occupation, and now, in 1817, he proposed a venture aimed at solving both his concerns. He sought, and obtained, his government's permission to establish a trading post on the southern coast of the Malay Peninsula, which lies immediately north and east across the Straits of Malacca from Sumatra and which separates the Indian Ocean from the South China Sea and the doorway to the Pacific. A site there would commercially and militarily command the Indian Ocean's eastern exit.

Raffles was well suited for the job. He had begun his Asiatic career as a "writer" for an independent English merchant doing business at the island of Penang off Malaya's west coast. He had traveled about the country and had read much about it, and he knew of a location that had once housed a thriving native city called Singa-pura. It was a small island just off the peninsula's southern tip. In 1818, he sailed there, found that Singa-pura was now a tumbledown native fishing village, made himself welcome, and, within a year, turned the place into a thriving trading post. It was ceded to the British by the local sultan in 1819 and, along with its surrounding patchwork of tiny islands—soon to be called the "Straits Settlements"—it became a Crown colony, first administered by the East India Company and then by the London government. In time, it became an important military base and the foremost trading center at the eastern terminal of the Indian Ocean, precisely as Raffles had anticipated.

Once a foothold was gained on the Malay Peninsula, British interests advanced northward to embrace the Penang and Malacca areas. Later in the century, because of fighting among the peninsula's several independent sultanates, the British government (it had by then, as we shall see later, taken over the administration of the Indian Ocean from the East India Company) sent in representatives to counsel the individual sultans and to bring peace. Called "residents," they succeeded on all fronts. Though always officially remaining in an advisory capacity, they became in actual practice the co-rulers of the sultanates. And, bringing peace, they opened up the peninsula to tin mining and rubber planting, boons to both the British and Malaysian economies. By the final decade in the century, the residents had their sultans working together on mutual problems, a sharp departure from the ancient tradition of warfare. Out of this cooperation was born the Federated Malay States, a union consisting of the Penang and Malacca settlements and four sultanates: Perak, Selangor, Negri Sembilan, and Pahang. Several sultanates remained out of the federation: Kedah, Kelantan, Perlis, Trengganu, and Johore. They were, nevertheless, under the British wing and were known as the Unfederated Malay States.

In developing its Empire, Britain exercised two types of control over its holdings: direct and indirect. In colonies where direct control was exercised, final authority came right from London. Under the indirect system, the British cooperated with native rulers or governments, operating in an advisory capacity and exercising their power through influence and the development of local loyalty to the Crown rather than via direct command. The Malay States, Federated and Unfederated, became a prime example of a successful venture in indirect control.

An ugly offshoot of trade with China earned Britain another possession along the India-Canton route. The widespread, and illegal, importation of opium into China by British merchants so infuriated Chinese officialdom that the Opium War of 1840 resulted. Britain emerged victorious and, as one of her winnings, was ceded the small island of Hong Kong, later acquiring nearby Stonecutter's Island and Kowloon Peninsula. Diminutive though the holding was, it was of vital importance to Britain; lying just eighty or so

miles from Canton, it stood as the last geographical link in
the protective chain along the India-Canton route, and in
time became one of the world's busiest seaports, bustling still
today. In 1898, to strengthen the holding, the London government leased for ninety-nine years a 356-square-mile
stretch of adjacent Chinese mainland coast, which subsequently came to be known as the New Territories.

The protective chain was completed in 1846 when the
British occupied the island of Labuan just off the west coast
of North Borneo and then established a colony in a section
of North Borneo itself. As Raffles had hoped little more
than a quarter century earlier, his nation's sea road to China
was adequately safeguarded against intrusion and her commerce and prestige at the eastern edge of the Pacific were
immeasurably enhanced.

Incidentally, five years before Labuan joined the chain,
an Englishman had won fame for himself on North Borneo.
He was an adventurer-seaman named James Brooke who, in
East India Company voyages to China, had landed at North
Borneo to be inspired with the idea of "civilizing" the natives there. He found the ruling sultan beset with a rebellion of tribes in the Sarawak region, joined the sultan in
quelling the insurgents, and was rewarded by being named
rajah of Sarawak. The British eventually drew his Sarawak
and neighboring Brunei under their wing, turning both into
protected sultanates and administering them in cooperation
with their rulers.

Steps, too, were taken in the 1800s to provide added protection to the passage between the Cape of Good Hope and
India. The British in 1839 established themselves at the sea-

port of Aden, which stands on the sandy point of land that
juts out into the Strait of Bab al Mandeb between the Gulf
of Aden and the Red Sea at the southwestern corner of
Saudi Arabia. The acquisition not only gave East India
ships a servicing station along the sea road to India but
activated a lively trade with the Arabs of the Red Sea. British control of Aden was, by cession or purchase, gradually extended for some miles along the southern coast of
Saudi Arabia and to the island of Perim lying in the Strait
of Bab al Mandeb.

Aden achieved its greatest importance with the 1869 opening of the Suez Canal, which thenceforth sent countless
ships of all nations out of the Mediterranean and down the
Red Sea to or past its docks. The port became a major
fueling station in the age of steam, a center of Asian trade,
and a militarily strategic point of immense value to the
British. Situated as it was, it served as a fulcrum of power,
affecting both the Indian Ocean and the Mediterranean.
On the one hand, it was part of the British Indian Ocean
holdings. On the other, thanks to the easy access made possible by the Suez Canal, it could, along with the Gibraltar
and Malta holdings, serve British power in the Mediterranean. Gibraltar had fallen into British hands during the
War of the Spanish Succession, and Malta during the Napoleonic campaigns; the former had been a Crown fortress
and colony since 1704, and the latter a self-governing colony
since 1814. Joining them later in the Mediterranean was the
island of Cyprus, which came under British administration
in 1876 and then was annexed to the Empire in 1914.

The final acquisitions of the period were made on the

Asiatic mainland—in India's neighbor to the east, Burma.

As early as the 1600s, the British and the Dutch had established a handful of minor trading posts on the coastal fringes of this exotic land whose upper regions stretch eastward to the borders of China and today's Laos, and whose southern area, thinning itself down to a narrow strip of land, runs down alongside Thailand to the Malay Peninsula. But neither group had ever been enthusiastic about the country. For both, it had loomed as a remote spot regularly torn by civil strife. And each had greater commercial preoccupations elsewhere—Indonesia for the Dutch, and India for the British.

The Dutch abandoned their Burmese posts before the end of the seventeenth century, but the British hung on until 1759, finally severing relations with the country when eight of their traders and one hundred Indian employees were slaughtered during a civil war. On two counts, though, the British soon tried to repair the break; they had awakened to the value of Burmese teak and, during the American Revolution, they feared that France was preparing to use Burma as a base for military operations against their holdings in India. The Burmese, however, refused to have anything to do with the English-speaking outsiders.

Then, beginning in 1819, with imperial designs of their own, the Burmese attacked and conquered the kingdom of Assam adjoining Bengal, slaughtered great segments of its population, announced their intention to take Calcutta, and started to make good the threat by marching southwest. British troops stepped into their path and, between 1824 and 1826, the first of three Burmese wars was fought. At its end, the victorious British were awarded Assam, the northwest Burmese territories of Manipur and Arakan, and, far to the south along the narrow strip of land adjacent to Thailand, the area of Tenasserim.

The win enabled the British to re-establish trading posts in Burma. They soon learned, however, that their ships were being subjected to mistreatment and extortion by the local officialdom whenever they put in at the port of Rangoon, which lies on the Bay of Bengal about midway along the country's north-south extent. To right the matter, the British fought the Second Burmese War in 1852 and were awarded the province of Pegu, which surrounded and stretched northward from Rangoon.

Finally, in 1885, the Third Burmese War was fought. Briefer even than the second and lasting only a matter of weeks, it centered itself on an independent kingdom in central Burma. On the surface, it concerned the imprisoning of the employees of a private English timber company by the local monarch after the firm had refused him a needed loan. Below the surface were other factors, chief among them a British desire for an overland trade route across the kingdom to China. The struggle ended with the British annexation of the domain, with the result that Britain now controlled all of Burma's most populous regions. The next years saw the country's last independent areas—the sparsely populated lands along its northern frontiers—placed in English-speaking care by treaty or cession.

The lands of the Indian Ocean and the eastern reaches of the Pacific were not all that were changed in the late eighteenth century and the first four decades of the nineteenth. In India, the East India Company itself had to endure change. It had to watch Parliament begin to take a hand in Indian affairs, so much of a hand that at last, following a series of disastrous events in 1857, the London government was able quickly to replace the company as the master of India.

Increased London interest in India began as soon as Clive gained control of Bengal. Hitherto, functioning as a commercial enterprise with a Crown charter, the East India operation had been outside parliamentary control. However, now that the company had gotten itself into the local political arena, Parliament wanted, and felt it only right to have, some control over its activities.

As a consequence, two parliamentary bills were enacted: the India Regulating Act of 1773 and the India Act of 1784.

The first created a governor-general for India and placed the three company headquarters there—Bombay, Madras, and Calcutta—under his authority, establishing his office at Calcutta. It made all his actions answerable to Parliament, the East India board of directors, and an advisory council of four members. The council, appointed by Parliament, not only had the right to advise him but also to overrule any of his decisions. On the surface, the whole arrangement seemed a simple one, but it actually put the governor-general in an intolerable position. He became a man with three bosses, an impossible role for any administrator to fill successfully.

The second bill attempted to improve the situation. It increased the powers of the governor-general to the point where he could now overrule his council so long as he put his reasons for doing so on paper. And it removed the company directors from a "boss" position, limiting their responsibilities to the management of company affairs. All that was placed over the governor-general was a London-based Board of Control, with a cabinet minister serving as its president. This approach to India's administration prevailed until London took over the country in 1858. At that time, the president of the Board of Control became the Secretary of State for India, and the Board itself the India Council.

Though it improved matters somewhat, the India Act did not clear the way for the efficient administration of the country. Indeed, it is likely that nothing but the harshest and most single-minded of dictatorships—and perhaps not even that—could have insured efficiency. There were simply too many factors conspiring against effectiveness in India: the greed that drove so many East India employees to seek the under-the-counter riches that Clive had found; the economic problems of running a company whose plant was sprawled over more than a million square miles of territory; the social problem of British snobbery toward the Indians. And there was the problem of an ancient Asiatic peoples being introduced swiftly to mysterious Western ways and even more mysterious Western developments.

Let us look at each in turn.

First, the problem of avarice: once Clive and his lieutenants had come home rich men, India became, more than ever before, a central attraction for adventurers in search of quick and fabulous wealth. They hurried out as East India writers, clerks, and officials to win their fortunes by taking advantage of everyone in sight, from the company itself and the greatest of native princes to the lowliest of Calcutta merchants. They dipped their fingers into tax revenues, first in Bengal and then elsewhere. They accepted bribes from local officials and traders in exchange for the advantageous pricing of cargo and the favoring of one trader over the other. And, as had been the case since the company's earliest days, they continued to trade independently on the side.

But the East India men alone cannot stand accused of the greed so rampant in the country. Many Indians themselves were just as much to blame. In Bengal, for instance, where the collection of taxes was left to the Indians and merely supervised by the British, it was an open secret that the collectors customarily raked off an extravagant amount for themselves and then paid off their overseers to keep their mouths shut. And, in the case of the assorted briberies, there always had to be two parties—the East India men being bribed and the Indians doing the bribing.

But make no mistake. The picture, as is any portrait of human frailty, was not all black. Not every East India man —not even many fortune hunters—treated the country selfishly or dishonorably. Clive himself, during his second and final tour as governor, tried to put the administration of Bengal on an honest footing. And his successor, Warren Hastings, did much to install an army of honest and efficient workers and managers in the company; they became the vanguard of the thousands of civil servants who, even at the worst of times, would serve with integrity and dedication during the British government's rule of India from 1859 to independence. Further, he made the British directly rather than indirectly responsible for the collection of Bengal taxes and ended—at least toward the close of his tenure—a major source of graft. Likewise, he cut down on the company's traditional commission system, always a source of corruption, and replaced it with inviting salaries for East India employees.

Incidentally, despite their efforts, both Clive and Hastings were in trouble when they returned to England. Their political enemies accused them of graft and mismanagement and brought them to trial. Clive, always the victim of a morose streak somewhere within himself, committed suicide in 1774, at the age of forty-nine. Hastings, after months of humiliation, proved his innocence.

Nor were all Britishers interested only in making money. Historian Gerald S. Graham notes that, so far as the nation's culture was concerned, Europeans quickly saw and made popular much Indian learning and sacred lore that was in danger of being neglected and forgotten. In the eighteenth century, British scholars began studying the Hindu civilization, a work that had nothing to do with administration or trade. Though burdened with many official duties, Warren Hastings took time to pursue an interest in sacred literature, and Edmund Burke (British writer and statesman who spent six years in India) developed a deep respect for "the piety of the Hindoos" and "for their holy religion and sacred functions." William Jones, a young English judge, accomplished much in revealing the treasures of Sanskrit literature. For ten years after arriving in India, Jones, who is called the founder of Indology, translated Hindu classics. He was working on a complete digest of Hindu and Moslem law at the time of his death in 1794.[9]

Professor Graham adds that, as early as 1791, the East

India Company sponsored the establishment of a Sanskrit college for the Indians.

Now, the excesses of the company itself: It not only winked its way around the sad practices of many of its employees, but, as Joe David Brown writes, in an effort to up its income, it devised land revenue systems that upset the age-old village economy of the country. For centuries, countless self-contained farms had dotted the Indian countryside and had been operated by hereditary landowners who paid an annual tribute—in the form of a portion of their crops— to princely overlords. In some areas, the British brought a new class of landlords into being. Called *zamindars,* they were given proprietary rights to the land in return for a fixed sum in taxes to be paid each year to the government. In other areas, the British required that peasants, known as *ryots,* pay high rentals to the state before their ownership of their land would be recognized. If they failed to pay, they were dispossessed. Their hereditary rights to the land were ignored.[10]

There is no doubt that the policy was stupid and grasping and that the dispossession of defaulters and the neglect of hereditary rights were inexcusable. But the company faced problems that, while certainly not pardoning it for its tactics, may put it more in the light of human blunderer than blackguard. To do business, it required hundreds of ships and thousands of employees. And to safeguard its interests in such a far-flung area, it required countless native troops, backed by a corps of British soldiers and officers. Its annual expenses were enormous and its annual losses from graft staggering. At one time in its history, it had been able to pay its investors annual dividends of no less than 200 percent, but, as growth and corruption accelerated hand-in-hand, it began to lose money. Strong remedies seemed mandatory to its board of directors. The circumstances suggest that the remedies may have been as much the decisions of desperate men as of villains.

Next, the matter of British snobbery: there is no doubt that many Britishers looked down on the inhabitants of India. They employed them as servants, dealt with them as traders, accepting their bribes, and trained them as soldiers. But they refused to live among them, preferring to install themselves in compounds that housed only their own kind. And they refused to steep themselves in the ways of the common people, choosing instead to socialize only—and on a very limited basis—with those of suitable means or status. That indeed the average Britisher saw the Indians, as well as all Asiatics, as his inferiors is seen in his oft-repeated and pious stance that they represented the "white man's burden." On the one hand, as was said at the beginning of this book, it suggested his sense of responsibility to better the lot of those whom he felt to be less advantaged than he, without the benefits of his civilization. On the other hand, it was the hallmark of an outrageous stuffiness. By what right did he feel that his civilization, his ways, and his outlook were superior to theirs?

And, to top all else, he was in India for the single purpose of enriching himself and his nation. Once his pockets were full, he would be on his way home and the country be damned. What other proof of condescension is needed?

His attitude was such that Sir Thomas Munro, the gov-

ernor at Madras, once acidly commented: "Foreign conquerors have treated the natives with violence and often
with great cruelty, but none has treated them with so much
scorn as we; none have stigmatized the whole people as unworthy of trust, as incapable of honesty, and as fit to be
employed only where we cannot do without them. It seems
to be not only ungenerous, but impolitic, to debase the character of a people fallen under our dominion." [11]

But, again, there are two sides to the story.

Certainly not all Britishers scorned the country. As Professor Graham writes, there were many Britishers—soldiers,
statesmen, and civil servants—who loved India, no matter
their weaknesses or mistakes.[12] Many, fascinated by the boiling life all about them, chose to remain there for the rest of
their days rather than run for home at the end of a tour of
duty. Others braved the ostracism of their kind by marrying
Indians. Many, like the celebrated Edmund Burke, were attracted to the nation's varied religions. And, assuredly, there
was no scorn in men such as Sir William Jones, the judge
who was drawn to the wonders and intricacies of Sanskrit
literature and Hindu and Moslem law.

Nor was the East India Company ever responsible for
that ultimate condescension: the deliberate attempt to
change India's way of life and its beliefs. Granted, there
was an early introduction of the English court system of
justice into the country and, as happened wherever Empire
went, a growing use of the English language, but, so far as
native customs and outlook were concerned, the company
policy was strictly a "live and let live" one. The company
was there to do business and it refused to shunt itself onto

the haughty—and, as it saw it, time-wasting—side track of enlightening the population. And so the sanctity of native practices was respected. Religious rites were left intact. No effort was made to Christianize the Indians or talk them out of their customs, many of which—among them *suttee,* the tradition that called for a widow to join her husband on his funeral pyre—the British found barbaric. The changes in such habits were wrought by missionaries who, caught in a religious fervor that was sweeping Britain, went out to India late in the eighteenth century.

But this is not to say that the country was without change. As the nineteenth century advanced to its midway point, English-speaking schools were established for the Indians. Irrigation systems were dug to increase the crop yield and improve the water supply. In 1854, the first railroad was put down in the country, to be operated by a private firm with London approval. These were changes that, as was pointed out earlier, prepared the nation, as perhaps the Indians by themselves could never have prepared it, for the technologically sophisticated twentieth century. But they were also changes that disturbed the indigenous population.

On that note, we now come to the last of the problems that made the administration of India so difficult: the Indian people themselves. In the mid-nineteenth century they were restless, troubled, ill-at-ease. They were a people slow to accept change, preferring their ancient heritage to the often blind rush toward the modern. The irrigation systems and their technicalities confused them. The roar of locomotives upset them, intruding as it did on the rural tranquillity that they so much admired and to which they had for ages past been accustomed. Wanting an education under any circumstances, they were willing to accept the English-speaking schools, but they resented the fact that their own language was being sublimated to a foreign tongue.

Further, they were by now impatient with the British presence. Too much of their country had fallen under the influence of the outsider. And the spread of that influence had caused too many local wars. And, while it fattened East India pocketbooks, it had brought starvation for native multitudes; the British system of land taxation had caused too many small farmers to lose their holdings to rich landlords who then grew even richer by planting such wanted trade crops as cotton and hemp in place of the rice needed to sustain the masses; from 1800 onward to the early twentieth century, famine played a regular and terrible role in the country, accounting for the loss of more than 32 million lives. Finally, there was anger at the missionaries who had begun arriving at the close of the eighteenth century. They were pushing hard to turn the people—Hindus, Moslems, Buddhists, Jainists, Sikhs, and Parsees alike—from their religions to Christianity. It was not only an annoying but, as the Indians saw it, an insulting effort.

The Indian's intrinsic reluctance to alter his old ways and the shredding of his patience by foreign elements not only contributed to the difficulties of British administration but also made the nation ripe for trouble.

And trouble came in 1857. It was triggered by what to many British eyes must have seemed the most inconsequential of circumstances: the issuance of a certain kind of rifle bullet to the nation's quarter of a million sepoy troops.

As historians Walter Phelps Hall and Robert Greenhalgh Albion explain the situation, the British army had replaced its old Sam Brown muskets with the more accurate Enfield rifles during the Crimean War (1853–1856). The muzzle-loading Enfields used a rifle cartridge consisting of a paper pouch that contained a powder charge. The pouch was fastened to the bullet, which was coated with grease so that it could fit easily into the rifle bore. When loading the rifle, a soldier gripped the bullet between his teeth, ripped off the paper, poured the powder into the rifle, and then rammed the bullet home. When the Enfields were issued to the sepoys, the rumor went round that the bullets were greased with beef or pork fat. The news infuriated the soldiers, who knew that the bullets had to be held in the mouth. Those sepoys who were Hindus regarded the cow as sacred. Those who were Moslems thought the pig was unclean. Both suspected a plot to make them outcasts from their religions and then turn them into Christians.

Hall and Albion go on to say that a number of sepoys with a cavalry regiment at Meerut, which is located near Delhi, refused issuance of the cartridges in April of 1857, whereupon they were brought to trial and sentenced to ten years in prison. Their comrades rebelled, freed them, and killed most of the regimental officers. Immediately, the revolt spread throughout the great valley of the upper Ganges. Sepoys at Delhi slaughtered many Britishers. At Cawnpore, a border station in Oudh, some four hundred Englishmen and eighty loyal Indians were attacked. They barricaded themselves behind a rough embankment and fought off several thousand sepoys for three weeks. They finally surrendered on the promise of safe conduct down the Ganges and away from the place. Then, as they were getting into boats to leave, they were massacred. About two hundred women and children were spared for the time being but, later, they were chopped to pieces and thrown down a well, just as a relief column was marching on the post. At the capital of Oudh, Lucknow, a force of about one thousand British soldiers, assisted by civilians and loyal sepoys, fought off attacks for two months until saved by reinforcements.[13]

The Sepoy Mutiny—or Indian Mutiny, as it was otherwise known—ended for all practical purposes in early 1858, though the final embers of the conflagration were not fully stamped out until the spring of 1859. The outbreak, lacking a strong central leadership and without the backing of most of the country's native rulers, was doomed from the start and was, in the main, restricted to areas of central and northern India, never reaching as far south as the British centers at Bombay and Madras. Once the uprising was quashed, British wrath fell hard on the mutineers. Several thousand were hanged, while many others were blown to bits from the muzzles of cannon. Historians Hall and Albion call the latter a particularly terrible punishment, for Hindu belief holds that bodies can never be put back together again for the future life.[14] Later, full amnesty was awarded to all sepoys who had not been leaders in the mutiny or who had not murdered British subjects.

Included on the list of the mutiny's casualties must be the East India Company, for the insurrection marked the end of its rule in India.

Ever since the Enabling Act of 1773, the London government had been taking an increasing hand in Indian affairs. There had long been the suspicion that the country was getting too big for the company to handle, and that its Indian Ocean monopoly was unfair to other British trading concerns and to the economy in general—a feeling that had led to the 1813 cancellation of the monopoly. Besides, there was much discontent at home over the company's behavior; especially obnoxious were the continuing tales of personnel graft and the land measures that had so wantonly disrupted the native economy. The mutiny put the cap on all the suspicion and anger. Now was heard the cry that any organization that could permit such an outrage to occur within its premises was not fit for the role of overseer.

Accordingly, the government divested the company of its authority and placed India in the hands of the Crown, with Queen Victoria adding "Empress of India" to her titles. The governor-general was renamed the Viceroy of India. The Board of Control became the India Council and its president the Secretary of State for India.

As it was extending its power, the company had come to govern sections of the country directly and to influence or supervise others through treaties or friendships with their local rulers. When Britain assumed control, it actually took over only those regions that had been directly governed by the company—regions that were immediately designated British India and that occupied about 60 percent of the nation's land and housed about 80 percent of its population. The remaining areas—the states of Baluchistan and Kashmir in the north, and Rajputana in the west, Mysore and Hyderabad in the south, and a stretch of central India—all submitted to British supervision; in some, the supervision was granted by friendly monarchs; in others, Indian aristocrats were installed as princes or kings on the proviso that they would cooperate with the British. The French were permitted to retain the few trading posts that had been left to them at the close of the Seven Years War. The posts would be finally handed over to London early in this century.

All arrangements for the passage of government from the company to the country were completed in 1858.

Added to the crown of Empire was the land that Britain would soon call her "brightest jewel." It would remain shining there until torn away in the twentieth century.

Chapter Eight

The Lion in the South

AFRICA IS THE world's second largest continent, exceeded in size only by Asia. Extending 5,000 miles from north to south, it occupies nearly 12 million square miles of the earth's surface and is home for approximately 305 million people.[15]

These peoples are divided into five principal ethnic groups: Arabs, who reside mostly in North Africa and Egypt; Hamites, who inhabit Ethiopia and much of the Sahara Desert; various black tribes, whose homelands are West Africa and the Sudan; Bantus, a race of natives who occupy central and southern Africa; and several aboriginal groups, among them the Pygmies of the Congo, the Hottentots of South-West Africa, and the Bushmen of Botswana's Kalahari Desert.

Their continent begins with a narrow strip of scrubland

along its northern shores. The scrubland runs to the Sahara Desert, which about a thousand miles farther south, gives way to a vast plateau, the most extensive tableland in the world. Built on ancient rock that, in some places, is believed to have been formed more than 300 million years ago, the tableland slopes gently from north to south and runs almost the full distance to Africa's southern tip. Plateaus and mountains rise out of it intermittently. It extends through broad grasslands, jungles, and rain forests, and it is cut in places by such broad river basins as those of the Congo and Nile.

More than 90 percent of the African people make their living at agriculture. Their crops are varied and include cotton, wheat, barley, olives, citrus fruits, tobacco, groundnuts, cocoa beans, cassavas, coconuts, bananas, dates, and cloves, most of which were introduced from other countries. Portugal, for example, gave the Africans citrus fruits, while the Arabs acquainted them with the date palm and the clove tree. Such commodities as cassavas, coconuts, the cocoa bean, tobacco, and bananas came from the Americas. Prior to the arrival of the foreigner, the Africans generally limited their crop output to millet and rice.

Grazing is an agricultural pursuit in certain parts of the continent. The Sahara nomads have cherished their flocks of goats for as long as they have traveled the region. Natives raise cattle in East Africa; goats and sheep in the Ethiopian, Tanzanian, and Congo highlands; while the white man grazes great herds of cattle in South Africa—cattle that, as we shall see, was responsible for the initial inland settlement of that area by Europeans. In the more remote regions, tribesmen continue to hunt for game as their ancestors did in the Stone Age. Fishing is done along all coasts, but the catch has traditionally been of little importance to the interior, for inland-bound shipments have usually been rotted by the heat before reaching their destinations, a situation that may improve with the increased use of refrigeration.

Mining, particularly in the southern areas of the continent, is widespread. Africa is a rich storehouse of mineral wealth, much of which has not yet been tapped to any consequential degree. Diamonds rank high among the resources of the Republic of South Africa, Tanzania, the Congo, and Angola. The Republic, likewise, works extensive iron and manganese holdings and contains—as do Rhodesia, Tanzania, and, far to the north and west, Nigeria—valuable coal deposits. Tin abounds in Swaziland, the Congo, Nigeria, and the Republic's Transvaal; and copper, zinc, lead, and uranium in Rhodesia and the Katanga region of the Republic of the Congo. Gold, which is to be had in several African areas, both in the north and south, has always been a prime resource of the Republic of South Africa's Orange Free State, with that region long accounting for about one-third of the world's gold supply. Oil and natural gas have been found in the Sahara and Libya.

Until well into our own century, Africa was called the "Dark Continent," a land whose geography, resources, and peoples were unknown to the outsider and thus steeped in mystery for him. The designation, however, could apply only to the continent's interior, for its coastal regions have been familiar to foreigners since the earliest days of Western civilization.

A portion of its northern coast was, five thousand years

ago, the setting for the great Egyptian civilization which welcomed traders from the Arab lands to the east and Sumer to the northeast. Then, in 600 B.C., departing via the Red Sea, the Phoenicians circumnavigated the continent, returning home through the Straits of Gibraltar or, as they were then called, the Pillars of Hercules. A century and a half later, Hanno of Carthage sailed west out of the Mediterranean and beat his way south to the Gulf of Guinea on the continent's distinctive bulge. He explored inland for a short distance, but abruptly turned back when he heard the uninviting sound of native drums. The Greeks followed Hanno and struck up a lively trade in African cloths and carvings.

As a matter of fact, several inland regions were also known to foreign ancients. The Greek explorer and geographer, Strabo, who lived between 66 B.C. and A.D. 24, hiked south through Egypt to Ethiopia, where, so he wrote, he saw half-naked blacks mining for gold, copper, and iron. Four centuries later, Christian missionaries entered Ethiopia to convert the natives, to note their ways, and to push on to the lands immediately beyond. And, later, far across the continent, the Arab explorer, Ibn-Batuta, who, so legend holds, traveled some seventy-five thousand miles in his seventy-three-year lifetime, made his way south from Tangiers to the cities of Timbuktu and Gao in what was to become West Africa. Here, in the ancient kingdom of Sornai, or Songhai, he found paved streets, tree-lined avenues, and breathtaking buildings, and a people who had founded great universities and had constructed for themselves a strict set of laws.

Africa was the first country to be visited by Europeans

during the Age of Discovery, and the knowledge assembled about it in early times should have been substantial enough to keep it from being the "Dark Continent" in their eyes. But, thanks to the Crusades of the eleventh century, they had forgotten most, if not all, of what had been so painstakingly learned about the continent. When they girded themselves and set out to free the Holy Land from the Turks, they looked on Africa as part of the Turkish domain. To them, it was a place to be ignored and avoided at all costs.

Consequently, when the Age of Discovery opened in the fifteenth century, Europeans knew little or nothing of Africa. They maintained but a single link with the continent: the Genoese and Venetian trade being conducted with Arab merchants along its northern coasts. To all the nations that approached Africa from the 1400s on, it was indeed a dark and mysterious land of strange peoples, strange tongues (at least sixteen major languages, each having a variety of dialects and pronunciations, with one native group—the Bantus —speaking some two hundred related languages and dialects), and strange diseases against which the newcomer had little or no resistance, diseases that struck him down with such regularity that more than one African area was grimly nicknamed "the white man's grave." The British were among the last to arrive in force on this alien scene, and among those to realize the greatest success there and to endure the longest.

When the Portuguese, on the orders of Prince Henry the Navigator, began probing south down the Atlantic toward the Cape of Good Hope in the 1400s, they had two aims in mind. The first, of course, was to breast the Cape and then make for the Far East. The second—and quite as important —was to set up a string of trading posts along the African west coast for the purpose of getting their hands on one of the continent's few known resources—gold.

Their series of southward thrusts, ultimately capped by Diaz's 1488 rounding of the Cape, brought them, in 1462, to the Gulf of Guinea on the underside of the continent's bulge. Here they began their trading efforts, first from their ships, then from the hulks of vessels that they anchored permanently in the shallows, and finally from shore stations, the first of which was built in 1481. While their explorer captains pushed on to and beyond the Cape, they ran up a profitable commerce with local tribesmen, stowing African gold in their holds in exchange for European silks, woolens, linens, brassware, rum, muskets, gunpowder, and household goods.

There was gold aplenty in the alluvial formations ashore, so much, in fact, that one stretch of gulf land became known as the "Gold Coast." But by the first quarter of the sixteenth century, the Portuguese had stumbled upon a new and even more profitable commodity. For years, Arab raiders had been swooping down on central and west African villages to steal their people away for the slave markets across the Red Sea. Now, with local potentates and chieftains serving as their highly paid henchmen, the Portuguese went into the slave trade, their markets being Europe and the New World. Soon, they were cramming no fewer than thirteen thousand hapless natives a year aboard their ships for transportation to such destinations as Spain, Jamaica, and Virginia.

And, just as soon, they were joined in Guinea waters by other nations, all eager for a share in both the slave and gold traffic, particularly the former. On hand were the Dutch, the French, the Danes, and the British. It is believed that British ships now and again had ventured down the west African coast as early as the 1430s, and the British are known to have been participating in the Guinea trade by the 1550s, but they did not establish their first trading posts ashore until late in the seventeenth century. By that time, they were involved in a human commerce stretching from the Gambia area on the western face of the bulge down to and beyond the mouth of the Congo River, with annual shipments that had risen from Portugal's early toll of thirteen thousand to more than seventy thousand for all the nations concerned. It is estimated that, during the lifetime of the trade, British slavers alone moved a cargo of approximately two million blacks out of their homeland.

Legally, the trade lasted until the early nineteenth century. Then the London government, taking its lead from Denmark and heeding the outrage of the average Britisher over the brutal traffic, outlawed it in 1807, with all the other participating nations following suit by 1836 and Britain abolishing slavery throughout the whole of the Empire in 1833. But the trade itself was much too lucrative to kill by legislative action alone. It continued illegally until late in the century, finally being wiped out altogether by alert coastal patrol measures—including forts on the Gambia River, one of the more crowded slave avenues from the interior to the sea—and a dying New World market.

Aside from the coastal trade, Britain displayed an apathy toward Africa from the sixteenth to the nineteenth century.

She allowed the Dutch to replace the Portuguese as the chief maritime power there (as they were doing in Indonesia) and let her concentration dwell far more on the Americas and the East India Company's gains in India. Seemingly content with her several trading posts, she evidenced little interest in the interior, neither establishing settlements nor sponsoring inland expeditions.

The apathy, however, was limited to the government. Many Britishers, as private citizens, found the continent a source of mounting fascination; in an age that marked the dawn of modern scientific thought, they were as curious about its wonders as they were about the transit of Venus that sent Cook to the South Pacific on the late eighteenth-century voyages that gained Australia and New Zealand for the Empire. Further, they sensed Africa's economic potential; assuredly it must contain resources that could be put to world-wide use. Sponsored by such private groups as the African Association and the Royal Geographical Society, they undertook in the eighteenth and nineteenth centuries a series of explorations to unravel its geographic mysteries. In great part, the investigations centered on Africa's principal rivers, with the explorers wanting to chart their full courses and assess their navigability for future commerce.

Between 1770 and 1772, Scotland's James Bruce made his way through the Ethiopian highlands and the neighboring Sudan to determine the course of the Blue Nile, that great inland branch of the Nile. Another Scot, Mungo Park, traced western Africa's Niger River from its inland reaches toward its mouth in the Gulf of Guinea in 1795 and again in 1805, on the latter journey reaching the Bussa rapids about three-quarters of the way to the Guinea coast. There, attempting to swim away from natives who had attacked his boat, he was drowned. His work was completed in 1830 when the English brothers, Richard and John Lander, worked their way past the Bussa rapids and proceeded the rest of the way to the coast. Then, in the nineteenth century, Richard Burton and John Speke, both of England, began their investigations of the Nile River, with Speke finally reaching its source in the area of Lake Victoria. Ultimately, the entire course of the mighty river was plotted by Germany's Heinrich Barth. Later in the century, such men as Germany's Hermann von Wissmann and English-born Henry Morton Stanley charted the Congo River in central Africa.

Exploration for the purpose of acquiring scientific knowledge and economic insight was not the only incentive that lured men to Africa. There were those who came as missionaries, intending to care for the physical ills of the natives, to convert them to Christianity, and to protect them from the dangers of the now illicit slave trade. One such missionary—Scottish-born David Livingstone—stayed on to become one of the continent's greatest explorers, if not its greatest. He visited the Kalahari Desert in 1849 and then moved north to the Zambezi River in the 1850s to befriend the people there and to chart the full course of the great river, which meanders from west to east across almost the full width of Africa's upper southern reaches. To the west, he found its beginnings in a small mountain stream. To the east, he followed it all the way to the coast, stopping en route to marvel at the magnificent Victoria Falls, and saw it empty into the Indian Ocean at a point opposite the island of Madagascar. Livingstone hoped to prove the river navigable all across the continent so that the inhabitants could transport their village wares along it to the outside world and thus strengthen their economy and make them more resistant to the raids of slavers. Later, he explored the Lake Tanganyika region and while there, during his famous meeting with Stanley, inspired the newspaperman-adventurer to turn his energies to African exploration.

All these explorations, bringing into sharp focus the fascinations of Africa and the economic opportunities available there, contributed much to British settlement. Other incentives developed later in the nineteenth century, among them the ambition of some government officials to expand the Empire, the desire of most to keep other foreign influences from gaining too much prestige on the continent, and the need of many an average Britisher to escape the crowded conditions and periodic economic depressions which had plagued the homeland since the 1600s. Over-population and stretches of widespread unemployment, as they had done in preceding times, drove thousands of Britishers to all points of the Empire during the nineteenth century. In one year alone, 1868–69, the total annual departures increased from 58,000 to 95,000 [16] with Africa receiving its fair share of the émigrés.

When the British finally overcame their apathy toward Africa, they established themselves in four areas: the South, the West, the East, and the Northeast.

In the South, they acquired the Cape of Good Hope in its entirety, which in the nineteenth century was divided into four states (the original Cape Colony, Natal, the Orange Free State, and the Transvaal) and three native regions (Bechuanaland, Swaziland, and Basutoland). The four states eventually formed the early twentieth century's Union of South Africa. South-West Africa, previously a German possession, was placed under the Union's administration by the League of Nations at the close of World War I.

In the West, they added Nigeria, the Gold Coast (now Ghana), Sierra Leone, and Gambia to the Empire, the first two facing on the Gulf of Guinea, and the third and fourth looking out on the Atlantic. Added to the western holdings at the close of World War I were portions of Togoland and the Cameroon, both League of Nations mandates.

In the East, they advanced into Southern Rhodesia, Northern Rhodesia, and Nyasaland, from there moving north to Kenya, Uganda, and Somaliland (now Somalia). Another German possession, Tanganyika (now Tanzania), came under their control when it was mandated to the League of Nations in the wake of World War I and then handed over to London for supervision.

In the Northeast, they came to hold Egypt and, under an agreement with the Egyptian government, the Sudan.

The history of the spread of British influence in Africa is a complex one, some military, some political, and all venturesome. The development of each area, often so distant in miles from its British-controlled companions, constitutes an individual story, though certain threads are common to all four accounts. For ease of reading, it is best to tell the story of each area separately. We begin at the southern tip of the continent.

South Africa

The British government secured its first foothold in southern Africa when, as was pointed out in the preceding chapter, it took over the Dutch settlement at the Cape of Good Hope and held it "in trust" for the Netherlands ruler—the pro-British William of Orange—when the French overran his country in the 1790s. London returned the colony to its Dutch owners in 1803, but occupied it again in 1806 to keep France from seizing it as a military base during the Napoleonic campaigns, this time holding it for good and acquiring the permanent rights to it in the international agreements that followed Bonaparte's collapse.

The British had little interest at the time in using the Cape (they christened it Cape Colony) as a springboard for expansion into the interior. Rather, as with Aden on the Red Sea and Mauritius in the Indian Ocean, they intended it primarily as a servicing station for India-bound ships and a strategic point for the military protection of their India sea route. But a single circumstance drove them to extend their hold deep inland within a few years: an immediate friction between themselves and the Cape's long-entrenched Dutch residents.

To understand the friction, it is necessary to take a look at the Cape's earlier Dutch history.

When they had first established themselves at the Cape (1652), the Dutch had done so with some two hundred men and an assortment of wives and children. The Dutch had wanted to use the site only as a servicing station—or, as they called it, a "refreshment station"—for their Indian Ocean ships, and the original settlers were dispatched there not to farm, mine, or build a colonial economy, but to install the station and then stand by to repair and supply food for the incoming ships. But soon the station people became interested in the land stretching northward into the interior. Physically less forbidding than many other African areas, it consisted of vast grasslands that invited farming and grazing, particularly the latter. It was an invitation that the newcomers could not resist. Then, after word of the agricultural possibilities there had reached the Netherlands and convinced the government that the Cape might become a valuable agrarian holding as well as a shipping convenience, the station personnel were joined, and ultimately absorbed, by an increasing number of "free burghers"—settlers who were the vanguard of the people soon to be called the Boers, a name that was eventually exchanged for Afrikaners—who were awarded free land to develop. These burghers numbered about twenty-five thousand at the time of the British acquisition in 1814 and had sprinkled the southern regions of the Cape with prosperous farms and cattle ranches.

From their first days in Africa, the Boers had imported slaves from Java and Madagascar to serve in their homes and work their lands. Then, as they had extended their holdings inland, they had encountered various native groups, all of whom resisted their advance. There were, first, the Hottentots, whom the newcomers enslaved. Then the Bushmen, whom they tried to obliterate, at one time even organizing forays against them that had the ugly smack of fox-hunting parties. And, finally, the Bantus, a great race of warriors whose various tribal branches savagely, and expertly, fought the intrusion until deep into the nineteenth century. Out of all these encounters there developed in the Boer a racial bigotry that haunts South Africa to this day. He came to look upon all black men as his inferiors, as ignorant and backward, as untrustworthy, and—after so many of his number had been felled by the Bushmen's poisoned darts and the Bantus' precision-aimed spears —as his enemy.

This bigotry was at the core of the trouble so quickly dumped on the British. The trouble erupted as soon as the British began introducing their own governmental functions at the Cape, particularly their courts of law. Hitherto, Cape justice had completely favored the Boer, based as it was on the simple premise that no black man's word was worth anything when set against that of a white man. The British now insisted on trials fairer to the rights of the natives. The new approach infuriated the Dutch. As they saw it, the newcomers were consorting with the enemy and defiling the white man's God-given privilege of superiority. Their fury reached its zenith in 1833 when Britain abolished slavery throughout the Empire. In Boer eyes this was an intolerable piece of foolishness in itself, and insult was added to injury when the British refused to compensate the Boers to the degree they thought adequate for the loss of their slaves.

Other developments worsened the situation. British missionaries arrived at the Cape and went to work to better the status of the blacks. The London government struck down the old Dutch practice of giving free land to settlers and replaced it with a system of land purchase through auction, a measure that struck hard at Boer pocketbooks. Next, Britain established English as the official Cape language and, in 1820, brought in some five thousand English-speaking settlers. Both actions led the Boers to fear for their cultural and economic survival. Finally, when a group of Boers rebelled against the new government, the British suppressed them with grim efficiency and executed five of their leaders.

There seemed to be only one bright spot in the whole picture. As was its usual colonial practice elsewhere, Britain granted the Cape colony partial self-rule, instituting a legislative council there in 1834. But even that development turned sour. When several Boer members of the council shoved through an anti-black measure, London flatly turned it down.

All these developments eventually proved unendurable for at least ten thousand of the Boer settlers. Beginning in about 1835 and continuing for a decade thereafter, they loaded their belongings into covered wagons and, driving their cattle and sheep before them, fled the Cape, striking deeper inland than ever before to seek a life beyond the reach of British authority.[17] The movement, which has gone down in African history as the "Great Trek," saw them extend the white man's grip northeast to the regions that are now Natal, the Orange Free State, and the Transvaal. Oddly enough, as we shall see, the Trek, which was made to escape the British, ended up by drawing them farther into the interior than they had ever planned to go.

The Trek was not made without a great toll in human life. In the Transvaal, the most distant region to be reached by the travelers, they encountered the fierce Matabele tribe, a branch of the Bantu family, who defended their lands in a series of attacks on the intruders. The *voortrekkers,* as they were called, in a strategy sure to remind any American of his West's nineteenth-century history, at first defended themselves by placing their wagon in *laagers* (tight and almost impenetrable circles); then, going on the offensive, they drove the Matabeles across the Limpopo River and out of the region.

In Natal, they came face to face with another Bantu tribe, the Zulus. They met them and soundly defeated them at the Blood River on December 16, 1838. But the Zulus were to remain a threat in both Natal and the Orange Free State for years to come. Their strength would not be broken until they met British forces in battle in 1877.

But despite the bloodshed and the arguments among Boer leaders—which caused some wagon trains to divide themselves into opposing factions, with each faction then setting out for its own destination—the *voortrekkers* settled themselves in the three areas. In each, they parceled out tracts of land for development and founded governments. Those who forded the Orange River at the Cape Colony frontier established the Orange Free State. Those who crossed the next river, the Vaal—which rises on the Orange Free State's western border to turn east for a run through the country's upper half—then pushed northward for another hundred miles or more and at last stopped in a land they christened the Republic of South Africa (its more common name was the Transvaal). And those who arrived in Natal over on the southeastern coast established the Republic of Natali. In each state, settlements, which eventually became great South African cities, began to take shape. The old native Port Natal started on its way to becoming today's Durban. The

roots of Bloemfontein in the Orange Free State were
planted, as were those of Johannesburg and Pretoria in the
Transvaal. The London government, though it still looked
on the *voortrekkers* as British subjects, declared that the
three states should be allowed to govern themselves. Accordingly, it granted independence to the Transvaal in 1852 and
to the Orange Free State in 1854, at the same time insisting
on retaining control of their foreign affairs. The handling
of Natal, as we shall see, proved to be a different matter.

By 1846, the Trek was all but a thing of the past. The
people at Cape Colony—including the many Boers who had
disapproved of the Trek from the start and had counseled
their friends to remain where they were and learn to co-
exist with the British—hoped that the matter was at an end
and that the colony could go about its business without further dissent. But subsequent events were to shatter their
hopes. Those events drew the British out from the Cape in
the wake of the trekkers and, in time, saw them acquire all
three states for the Empire.

The first move was made in Natal. Prior to the arrival
of the trekkers, the British had made inroads into Port
Natal, establishing a base there. The site was regarded as
an important link in the Britain-India sea route and, as soon
as the Republic of Natali was formed, the British decided
that their hold on the port was in jeopardy. Consequently,
Cape Colony annexed the newborn republic in 1843. Nine
years later, it was designated a British colony. The annexation caused many of the *voortrekkers* there to turn tail and
drive their wagons back into the Orange Free State on the
west or blaze a trail north into the Transvaal.

The next move came in 1867, when gold was discovered

in the Kimberley area on the Orange Free State's western frontier. At the time, the border between the State and the adjoining vast land, which belonged to the Bechuana tribe, was only dimly defined. The tribal territory, known as Bechuanaland, (now Botswana), had already received some British settlers and missionaries, among the latter the renowned Dr. Livingstone, causing the Cape Colony to feel that it had a claim on the land. Now the Cape's leaders argued that the diamond-rich Kimberley region was actually within Bechuanaland and so rightfully belonged to their colony. The Orange Free State, of course, disagreed. A long wrangle ensued. It ended with the Kimberley field in Cape hands and with the Orange Free State being compensated ninety thousand pounds for its loss—an inconsequential sum when compared with the riches that were to pour from it for years, continuing even today.

Despite such periodic difficulties, the development of Cape Colony and Natal proceeded smoothly during the latter half of the nineteenth century. The Cape grew in importance as an agricultural region and its chief port, Capetown, became the central embarkation point for diamonds from the Kimberley field, while Durban in Natal developed as a vital port for the Indian Ocean trade. Exactly twenty years after being given its first legislative council, Cape Colony was granted a bicameral parliament and a prime minister in 1854, and then full jurisdiction over its internal affairs in 1873. Complete internal self-government followed in Natal in 1892. The effects of Lord Durham's Canadian recommendations—the Magna Carta of Empire—were being felt in Africa.

In the Transvaal, however, turmoil seemed to be the order of the day. Boer factions fought each other for political control there. The small republic looked covetously at the Orange Free State and even went so far as to attempt a minor invasion to bring the region under its wing. And there was always the danger that, to weaken the British hold on South Africa, the Transvaal Boers might welcome relations with other European nations now entering Africa. In an attempt to quiet the whole situation, in 1877 London ordered that the Transvaal be annexed to Cape Colony and sent in troops to back up the decision. It was a measure that failed to work. The Boers rose in revolt, defeated the intruder forces in the battle of Majuba Hill in early 1881, and reclaimed their independence.

Then, making matters worse, in 1886 gold was discovered in the Transvaal, near Johannesburg, resulting in a flood of adventurers from Britain, the United States, Australia, Canada, and continental Europe. The newcomers, threatening the rural way of life that the Transvaal cherished, infuriated the Boers. At first, they hoped that the gold rush would prove a transient phenomena, but instead they had to watch the formation of giant mining firms and the *Uitlanders* (outsiders) settle down to stay. Under their president, Paul Kruger, the Boers did all in their power to make the newcomers unwelcome. They overcharged them for mining supplies; they levied heavy tolls on gold shipments; and, in their strongest move, they denied them the right to the vote.

The situation was watched closely from the Cape, particularly by one man, Cecil Rhodes. Among the most notable figures in South African history, he was at the time prime minister of the Cape Colony. In common with a growing number of London legislators and officials, he wanted to see all of South Africa unified. To him, unification meant a logical and advantageous pooling of resources. Further, and of even greater importance, unification would create a political and geographical fortification for the protection of British interests against intrusion by other nations now securing substantial footholds on the continent. Germany was presently close by in South-West Africa and, to the north, in Tanganyika. France was in western Africa and the Sahara. Belgium was in the Congo. Without a unified front and with the Transvaal Boers free to deal with whomever they wished, the road to foreign penetration into the South might be all too easily opened. And, finally, unification would constitute a significant step toward the realization of a dream that Rhodes, who had early identified the economic value of all Africa to Britain, had long cherished. He wanted to see a British Empire from Cape Colony straight up through east and central Africa to Cairo.

In the Transvaal situation, Rhodes glimpsed the chance for unification, though realizing that it would be forced unification. If the situation could be made to get completely out of hand, he could legitimately move into the Transvaal under the guise of restoring peace while actually taking control of the country. To achieve that goal, he planned an uprising within the Transvaal, scheduling it for December 28, 1895.

Rhodes, who was forty-three years old at the time, had come to South Africa in the 1860s and had joined in the diamond rush to the Orange Free State. A tough businessman with an eye for unfolding opportunities, he had, by the age of thirty-five, become one of the world's richest men, having obtained control of the Kimberley diamond mines. From the world of finance, he moved into politics, winning the support of both Boers and Britishers at the Cape with his stand that the colony should have full self-government. He was known as a fair-minded man, but, in his march to personal wealth and political prominence, he had acquired a number of hard, venturesome aides. Now, plotting the uprising, he turned to one of them—Leander Starr Jameson —for help. He assigned Jameson to the command of a force of private police (all in Rhodes's pay) that would invade the Transvaal from adjoining Bechuanaland and join the insurgents in seizing Johannesburg and deposing President Paul Kruger.

The intricately conceived plot misfired, however. The uprising was canceled at the last moment because of dissension among its leaders. But by that time Jameson was in Bechuanaland with five hundred men. Without consulting Rhodes, he decided to press his attack, hoping that he could revitalize the revolt. He and his small force crossed the border on December 29, 1895, and five days later were surrounded by Boers and made to surrender. The British government, embarrassed and enraged by the plot, sentenced Jameson and five of his officers to a fifteen-month prison sentence. Jameson outlived the humiliation and reentered South African politics to become the Cape's prime minister in 1904. The plot ruined Rhodes's political career, forcing his resignation as prime minister. He died seven years later.

The raid and the plotted uprising brought relations between the Cape and the Transvaal to a seemingly intolerable point. But matters managed to worsen during the next few years. The British, still maintaining control of the Transvaal's foreign affairs, demanded that President Paul Kruger give the *Uitlanders* the vote. Realizing full well that the outsiders now outnumbered the Boers and that the franchise would mark the end of Boer political supremacy, he flatly refused. Then he appealed to Germany for diplomatic help to try to persuade Britain to change its mind. This made Britain aware of the threat of German influence in South Africa. She immediately strengthened her army there. Kruger demanded that the new troops be sent home, a demand that went ignored. Kruger, fearful that his country would soon be invaded, decided to strike first. Boer regiments marched south into British territory. War was declared on October 12, 1899.

The ensuing conflict—known variously as the South African War, the Anglo-Boer War, or, simply, the Boer War—continued until May of 1902, with the Orange Free State aligning itself with the Transvaal and the British committing no fewer than 450,000 men to the struggle; among them were troops from Canada, New Zealand, and Australia, marking the first time that her overseas holdings had fought on behalf of the mother country. Successful in their initial attacks, the Boers were effectively defeated by early 1900 when British forces captured Bloemfontein in the Orange Free State and Pretoria and Johannesburg in the Transvaal. Fighting continued for another fifteen months, however, with the Boer forces dividing themselves into guerrilla bands that harassed British railways, roadways, and garrisons.

When peace was restored on May 31, 1902, British authority reigned supreme in both the Transvaal and the Orange Free State. However, Britain, acting on the same impulses that were guiding her in the handling of many of her other overseas possessions, quickly restored full internal government to both regions—to the Orange Free State in 1906 and to the Transvaal in 1907. It was a generous move, evidencing both the liberality of the London government and its faith in the Boers, and the Boer leadership responded accordingly. Jan Christiaan Smuts and Louis Botha, who, just a few years earlier, had been such formidable British enemies, joined with Natal and Cape Colony representatives to plan the move that the Cape had sought for so long—the unification of South Africa. In 1908, they met at Durban to frame the South Africa Act. The Act was sent to London, where it was reviewed and enacted into law by Parliament in 1909. It called for the Union of South Africa to come into existence on May 31, 1910.

Of the Act, writer Tom Hopkinson remarks that the new Union, taking shape so soon after the war, was seen as a fine act of statesmanship that would bring the British and the Boers together and see them launch an era of cooperation. "The Constitution is not man's work," General Jan Christiaan Smuts observed. "It bears the impress of a Higher Hand." [18]

Joined in the Union were Cape Colony (now to be called Cape Province), Natal, the Orange Free State, and the Transvaal, comprising in all an area of 471,442 square miles. The Union was to be governed by a parliament and a prime minister, with the first man to hold that office being Louis

Botha. It was to have three seats of government: Capetown, the legislative capital; Pretoria, the administrative capital; and Bloemfontein, the judicial capital.

Within the Union's geographical boundaries were three native states: Bechuanaland, Swaziland, and Basutoland. On the insistence of the London government—chiefly because of its dislike of the anti-black sentiment that had now become traditional with most South African whites, Britisher and Boer alike—the trio was permitted to remain independent of the newborn federation. Two had become protectorates and one a colony within the Empire by the time of unification and they were now retained as such. Bechuanaland had been made a protectorate in 1885 after repeated border skirmishes between its natives and Orange Free State settlers. Swaziland had been administered by the Transvaal between 1894 and 1907, at which time its supervision was entrusted to a British commission. Basutoland had come under British protection as early as 1868, thanks to white-black friction there, and had been designated as a colony in 1884.

The Union and the native states remained within the framework of Empire and then of Commonwealth until deep into the twentieth century. The direction that each then elected to take is a story to be told in Chapter Eleven.

East Africa

Lying north of the Transvaal is a land that was known to outsiders as Zambezia, when Africa was still the "Dark

Continent." It is a vast tract of more than 486,000 square miles that stretches from the Transvaal frontier to and far beyond the Zambezi River. In the late years of the nineteenth century, British settlers and miners came there, planning to transform its wilds into ordered farm lands and burrow into its soil for a long-suspected largesse in mineral wealth. In time, the lands south of the Zambezi River became Southern Rhodesia, while those north of the river were designated Northern Rhodesia and Nyasaland—the Rhodesias so-named in honor of Cecil Rhodes.

Zambezia, according to the finds of archaeologists, is known to have been occupied by Africans since the fourth century B.C. The Bantus, coming in from somewhere to the north in search of fresh hunting and grazing lands, are believed to have arrived during the fifteenth century. By the nineteenth century, a variety of Bantu tribes (chief among them the Bembu, the Lozi, and the Tonga) controlled the region north of the Zambezi River, while the Matabele (who fought the first *voortrekkers* in the Transvaal) were in force south of the river, having overcome and enslaved the Shona peoples, who had occupied the area for centuries. And, also by late in the century, the Zambezi had been explored along its full length by David Livingstone, Zambezia itself had witnessed an attempted settlement by the Portuguese, and both its northern and southern regions had developed a native trade with neighboring Mozambique to the east and Tanganyika to the northeast.

It was to the area south of the Zambezi River that the British first came. In 1889, Cecil Rhodes, having built his fortune in Bechuanaland's Kimberley diamond area, turned

his eye to Zambezia and formed the British South Africa
Company, its purpose to be the development of agricultural
and mining operations there. In the company, he also saw
the opportunity to further his dream of a Cape-to-Cairo
British Empire in Africa. An economic advance into Zambezia would carry him one more giant step along the road
to the realization of that ambition.

A year later, armed with a treaty signed by the Matabeles,
he sent in his first contingents of settlers and prospectors
under the command of Leander Starr Jameson. They established themselves far to the south of the Zambezi, only
to meet with disappointment, for the land there revealed
no significant mineral content and was unsuitable for the
raising of good crops. Joined by other settlers and miners,
the whites began to push toward the river regions, where
the Matabeles were to be found in greatest strength. Regardless of the treaty with Rhodes, the Matabeles resisted
the influx, which they saw as threatening their survival, and,
from 1893 to 1897, fierce fighting between the blacks and
whites was the order of the day. The worst incident in the
struggle occurred early in 1896 when the Matabeles overran
white farms and towns, slaughtering hundreds of Englishmen. It was an attack decided upon when Jameson and his
five hundred South Africa Company policemen departed for
the ill-fated Johannesburg raid and left the Zambezia settlers unguarded.

Rhodes, disgraced by the Transvaal plot, regained some
of his prestige by traveling to Zambezia and negotiating a
peace treaty with the Matabeles. It was a treaty that, with
the exception of sporadic bickerings over land rights here

and there, brought lasting peace to the south-of-the-river region, which by then was called Southern Rhodesia. For the next quarter of a century, the South Africa Company administered the region.

The native tribes of the northern area asked to be placed under British protection in 1891 as a safeguard against the forays of Arab slave traders, a request that the anti-slavery London government was pleased to grant. The area was divided into Northern Rhodesia and Nyasaland, the latter becoming a protectorate on the eastern frontier, and the administration of both was entrusted to the South Africa Company in 1899. It was a responsibility that the company held until 1923, at which time the administration of Northern Rhodesia and Nyasaland passed to the Crown and Southern Rhodesia became a self-governing colony. In 1953, the two Rhodesias and Nyasaland formed themselves into the self-governing Federation of Rhodesia and Nyasaland. The later twentieth-century political activities of these states will be dealt with in Chapter Eleven.

By the autumn of the nineteenth century, all European eyes had come to look covetously at Africa, now that exploration and beginning white exploitation had unveiled some of its myriad wonders and commercial possibilities. Europe, thanks to its many wars and to the over-production of its by now industrialized nations, was struck with an economic depression in the 1870s. To develop new markets for their products and to find new lands for settlement by their overcrowded homeland populations, seven countries began to compete for the acquisition of African territories. Theirs was a southward rush that, by 1900, saw the entire continent—with the exception of Morocco, Ethiopia, and the Boer-held Transvaal and Orange Free State (the South African War was yet to be concluded)—under the wing of foreign powers.

It was as a participant in this rush that Britain secured her next East African areas, Kenya and Uganda. In the early 1880s, she and Germany began to compete for trade along the Kenya and Tanganyika coasts. The two nations, wisely, were far more eager to concentrate their efforts on developing a profitable commerce than to waste time bickering over territorial rights; consequently, in 1886, they reached an agreement that gave each a sphere of influence in which to work, further refining these spheres in an accord of 1890. Britain took for her sphere the region along the Kenya shores, while Germany accepted Tanganyika to the south. As a result of the agreement, an association of British merchants in 1887 leased for trade development a strip of the Kenya coast that was controlled by a local sultan, Barghash, from his headquarters on the offshore island of Zanzibar. A year later the merchants transformed themselves into the Imperial East Africa Company and secured a charter from the Crown. But their company lacked the funds to develop the area properly and so, in the 1890s, its franchise was surrendered to the London government, with little Zanzibar becoming a protectorate in 1890 and Kenya, whose soil promised both mineral and crop wealth, becoming the East African Protectorate in 1895. Britain encouraged settlement of the country, a maneuver that eventually rewarded her with a wide variety of crops—ranging from corn, coffee, and tea to wheat, rice, sugar cane, and casavva—and with mineral resources that included petroleum and soda ash. The government also promoted expansion and development by completing a railroad from Mombasa on the coast to Lake Victoria deep inland. In 1920, the protectorate, comprising an area of 224,959 square miles, became both the Crown colony and protectorate of Kenya. The Crown colony occupied the inland regions while the protectorate embraced the coastal strip originally leased from the sultan Barghash and now ruled jointly by his successor and the government, although, in practice, the present sultan's rule was in name only.

Adjoining Kenya on the west was the Uganda region, inhabited by several Bantu tribes. A land of mountains, plateaus, grasslands, and tropical rain forests, it was declared a British sphere of influence in the 1890 refinements of the Kenya-Tanganyika agreement. Previously, it had been assigned to Germany, but was given to Britain in return for the North Sea island of Helgoland, which the British had held since the Napoleonic campaigns.

Four years after receiving the region, Britain declared it a protectorate. In its southeastern corner, Uganda proved to be a fertile farming area, capable of such crops as bananas, coffee, tea, sugar cane, and rice. Its Ruwenzori mountain range was found to be rich in copper, tungsten, cobalt, and gold.

Actually, the area that was designated a protectorate in 1894 constituted only a portion of what eventually became today's Uganda. Assumed by the British at that time was an eastern border region occupied by the Baganda natives and called by them Buganda. Later, three other native kingdoms deeper into the interior joined the protectorate, extending the British holding toward its eventual geographic limits. Uganda's ultimate limits of 93,981 square miles were not fully defined until 1923.

British acquisitions in East Africa were completed with the securing of a portion of what is now the nation of Somalia (then known as Somaliland) and with the post-World War I receipt of administrative control of Germany's Tanganyika. The latter was a responsibility given to London by the League of Nations.

With a coastline of 1,837 miles, Somalia today occupies 246,000 square miles and extends northward along the Indian Ocean from Kenya to the Gulf of Aden, where it turns westward for a run to the Straits of Bab el Mandeb at the entrance to the Red Sea. From the 1860s on, it was the target of three European nations. France was the first of the trio to arrive on the scene, establishing a small colony on the west side of the straits and christening it French Somaliland. The British, whose East India Company had installed trading posts on several offshore islands as early as 1840, landed next. Starting in 1884, they occupied towns along the northern coast and, thanks to a series of treaties executed with local tribes, were able by 1887 to turn most of the upper half of the country, with the exception of the French holding, into the Protectorate of British Somaliland. Italy was the third nation to appear, her date of arrival being 1885. She, too, began by settling herself in a series of towns to the south of the British domain, and eventually extended her claims throughout Somalia's southern reaches.

The country—inhabited principally by nomads, capable of producing just a few crops, and able even today to export little more than bananas, hides, skins, and livestock—was never considered by the British to be a holding of economic significance. Rather, they saw it chiefly as a station for maintaining their influence in the Red Sea—which had emerged as such a vital avenue for all European-Asian trade since the completion of the Suez Canal in 1869—for British Somaliland lay just a few miles across the Gulf of Aden from the strategic Aden holding at the southern entrance to the Red Sea. Furthermore, their presence kept the French and Italians from growing so powerful in the region that they would pose a threat to the security of the Aden holding.

The little protectorates, however, gave the British a goodly share of trouble. For the first two decades of the twentieth century, the Somalia tribes attacked and harassed the whites in their midst in an unending and ultimately unsuccessful attempt to evict them. Then, in 1940, during World War II, Italian forces invaded the protectorate and captured it, only to be driven out within a year and to sacrifice their own Somalia regions to the British. The British held Italian Somaliland until 1950, at which time it was returned to Italy on the understanding that it be held for ten years only and that, during that time, its peoples be readied for independence. To the north, the British joined in the program leading to independence. In mid-1960, both areas began life on their own—the British sector on June 26 and the Italian region on July 1. The French continued to hold the small colony they had established just a century earlier.

West Africa

Not only the advance of other European nations into Africa but also Britain's early distaste for the slave trade accounted for her acquisitions in western Africa. Located on the continental bulge and the first regions to feel the presence of European ships in the dawning days of the Age of Discovery, they numbered four in all. They were Gambia and Sierra Leone on the Atlantic, and the Gold Coast and Nigeria on the Gulf of Guinea.

Gambia is today one of the world's smallest countries, consisting of just 4,003 square miles. Finger-shaped, it pokes its way into the continent for about two hundred miles, is surrounded on three sides by the nation of Senegal, has an Atlantic frontage measuring no more than thirty miles, and is as narrow as fifteen miles across at certain inland points. Its principal geographic feature is the Gambia River which runs the length of the country, flowing in from Senegal after leaving its source in the Futa Jallon Mountains of Guinea.

The Portuguese, in their patient thrusts southward to the Cape of Good Hope, were the first Europeans to put in at the Gambian coast, Alvise da Cadamosto having dropped anchor there in 1455. The British became involved in Gambia's developing gold and slave trade in the late 1500s and, early in the next century, began to probe up the Gambia River to explore the interior, establishing several fortress trading stations along the shores and on mid-stream islands as they went. They seemed content with their coastal trade and likely would not have furthered their inland ventures beyond mere explorations had not two circumstances forced them to a change of mind.

First, there was the matter of slavery. Today, Gambia's chief export is its peanut crop, but three hundred years ago its Gambia River served as one of West Africa's major thoroughfares for hauling slaves down to the Atlantic coast from the deep interior. When Britain outlawed the trade in 1807, she manned her fortress trading posts with patrol units that maintained a constant—and highly successful—watch for slave cargoes being smuggled down the river. Her vigilance won her the respect of the surrounding natives and made her something more than a coastal trading customer—made her, in fact, a watchdog over the entire country's welfare. It also led to the second circumstance that contributed to her growing inland influence.

At the time, Gambia was occupied by five tribal groups who were constantly at war with each other. Several of the chiefs, tired of the fighting and fearful of seeing their tribes destroyed, sought the protection of the admired British in their river fortresses. In response, the British took over the administration of the little country, later designating it a Crown colony (1843) and then converting it into a colony and protectorate in 1866. The colony embraced only the city of Bathurst on the Island of St. Mary's at the mouth of the Gambia River, while the status of protectorate was awarded to the whole of the interior.

In the end, the dual circumstances proved advantageous to Britain. In the late 1800s France entered and took control of adjoining Senegal. The British presence in Gambia prevented the French from gaining access to the final Atlantic-bound miles of the Gambia River and deprived them of a vital West African trading center at its mouth.

Sierra Leone, today a country of 27,699 square miles, lies southeast of Gambia on the bulge and is bordered on one side by Guinea and on the other by Liberia. Pedro de Cintra was the first Portuguese captain to come ashore there, arriving in 1462. He is the man credited with christening the mountainous land Sierra Leone, which means "Lion Mountains." The country soon became a center of the slave trade but, in 1787, its slave history took an odd turn.

That was the year in which an Englishman named Granville Sharp began to work. Violently opposed to slavery, he gathered some four hundred freed American slaves under his leadership and established for them a colony at the point on the Sierra Leone coast where the city of Freetown now stands. The small colony, after a start that was marked by starvation, illness, and attacks by inland tribes, survived and flourished. The British contributed to its development after the slave trade was outlawed. Whenever British patrol boats intercepted a smuggler ship and unchained its human cargo, the released natives were carried to Freetown, where they had the choice of making their way home or settling down as free men.

The British declared the coastal region around Freetown a Crown colony in 1808. Then, with the arrival of France in the West African interior, they spread their influence into the interior, finally designating the inland area a protectorate in 1896. Both the colony and the protectorate remained as British holdings until 1961.

Ghana is today a country occupying 92,100 square miles on the Gulf of Guinea, but in its early days of European exploitation it was known as the Gold Coast, a name given it because of the great amounts of the sought-after metal found in the alluvial formations just inland of its shores. The

Portuguese reached Ghana in 1471, christened it with its original name, built up a lively trade in gold and slaves, and were driven out by the Dutch in 1642. With the outlawing of the slave trade, the British eventually replaced the Dutch there and, due to the inland work of missionaries, early exerted a cultural influence on the country. The coastal region was made a Crown colony in 1874 and the two major inland areas—one a chunk of country belonging to the Ashanti tribe and the other called the Northern Territories —were established as protectorates in 1901.

The largest of the West African holdings acquired by Britain proved to be Nigeria, which rises along the eastern reaches of the Gulf of Guinea and spreads inland to cover some 357,000 square miles. With the arrival of Europeans in the Age of Discovery, it became, in common with its companion states, a mecca for slave traders. After 1807, Britain emerged as the dominant trading nation there, helping to establish palm oil as the country's new chief commodity for export. In 1861, she declared the coastal city of Lagos, which is located near the country's western border, a Crown colony. Then, in an effort to settle tribal wars and to forestall possible French infiltration, she created two major inland holdings in the 1880s—the Protectorate of Southern Nigeria and the Protectorate of Northern Nigeria. Both remained separate domains until 1912, at which time they were combined and administered through a collection of native chieftains. Tribal jealousies in the country's eastern sector, however, ultimately rendered the arrangement unworkable, causing the British to assume direct authority over all Nigeria, an authority that it held for three decades while, at the same time, granting the Nigerians increasing degrees of self-government.

In addition to its four acquisitions, Britain was awarded two West African territories in the post-World War I years —portions of Togoland and the Cameroon.

The former, a narrow strip of land now simply called Togo, lies immediately east of Ghana and was claimed by the Germans in 1884. Gold Coast troops, aided by French forces, invaded and captured the country shortly after the outbreak of hostilities in 1914 and held it until war's end, at which time it became a League of Nations mandate and was placed with the British and French for administration.

By 1914, the Cameroon, immediately adjoining Nigeria on the east and south, had been a German holding for thirty years. It, too, became a League of Nations mandate and, likewise, was entrusted to the care of both France and Britain. The former assumed responsibility for 80 percent of its territory, while the latter attended to the remaining 20 percent.

Later, in the 1940s, both Togoland and the Cameroon became United Nations trusteeships.

The mid-twentieth century stories of the western holdings will be told in Chapter Eleven, along with those of British possessions elsewhere in Africa.

Northeast Africa

Neither the fight against slavery nor the fear of intrusion upon their African interests by European competitors brought the British into Egypt. Responsible, rather, was the Suez Canal.

The one-hundred-mile-long waterway was built by a French firm, the Suez Canal Company, and, begun in 1859, required ten years to complete. Egypt invested heavily in the company and, according to the terms of the construction agreement, granted to it the privilege of operating the canal for ninety-nine years, with Egypt having a share of the profits. It was an arrangement that both displeased and troubled Britain, for it meant that the new and much shorter water route to her Indian Ocean holdings was to be in foreign hands. She saw the chance, however, to remedy the situation when, in 1875, she learned that Egypt was tottering on the brink of bankruptcy, thanks in part to her heavy investment in the canal company and in equal part to her careless spending policies in other economic areas. Britain, at the urging of Prime Minister Benjamin Disraeli, capitalized on the situation by purchasing Egypt's share in the canal company. Then, when Egypt, despite the British purchase money, went into bankruptcy anyway, Britain joined with France to supervise her financial affairs.

Because of these two fortuitous circumstances, Britain gained not only a say-so in the doings of the canal but a foothold in Egypt as well. In a matter of months, she was alone in Egypt, for, when she and France found it difficult to work together, she persuaded the French to leave Egypt in her hands while they concentrated on developing their interests in Morocco. Her hold on the country was then strengthened by an Egyptian revolt in 1881. Egypt at the time was—and had been since 1517—a domain of Turkey's

Ottoman Empire, and the uprising was intended to evict the khedive, the Ottoman ruler there, and return the nation to native control. Britain immediately sided with the khedive, stamped out the rebellion, and became the close associate of the grateful ruler in operating the government until World War I. The war completed the process of acquisition, for Turkey chose to side with Germany in the struggle, and Britain promptly reacted by installing additional troops in Egypt and declaring it a protectorate. Throughout the war, her army and navy guarded the Suez Canal, preventing its use or destruction by enemy forces.

The Anglo-Ottoman friendship that resulted from the revolt of 1881 extended British influence southward to the vast region known as the Sudan. Encompassing an area that spreads its way through deserts, grasslands, and rain forests for a total of 967,500 square miles, the Sudan is Africa's largest country. With a history dating back to the days when ancient Egyptian pharaohs carted off huge amounts of its gold deposits, it was conquered by the Ottoman's khedive in 1821. Consequently, when the revolt of 1881 erupted inside Egypt, it likewise broke out in the Sudan. Here, however, it met with success. Continuing until 1889, the uprising caused the eviction of both the Egyptians and their British allies. It was an eviction that lasted until 1898, at which time a combined British-Egyptian force reconquered the region. A year later, Britain and Egypt declared the region a joint protectorate, or a condominium, as the arrangement came to be called. Under the terms of the dual administration, Britain appointed a governor general and all major government officials to the region, with Egypt reserving the right to approve them. For years to come, the great area was to be known as the Anglo-Egyptian Sudan.

With the acquisition of Egypt as a protectorate and the Sudan as a condominium, the extension of British influence in Africa was completed. Extending northward through the Union of South Africa, the Rhodesias, Tanganyika, Kenya, and Uganda to the Sudan and Egypt, buttressed on the east by British Somaliland, on the west by Gambia, Sierra Leone, the Gold Coast, Nigeria, Togoland, the Cameroon, and South-West Africa, the British Empire indeed stretched from the Cape to Cairo.

Cecil Rhodes's dream had become a reality, and the lion in Africa stood in the full sun of noon. But, even as he stood in the noontime of his power, the day was beginning to wane. The mid-twentieth century was fast approaching. With its upheavals and the changes in attitude that it wrought throughout the world, it brought him to the sunset of Empire.

Chapter Nine

Transformation: Ireland

THE EARLY TWENTIETH century saw the British Empire come to full flower, reaching its zenith at the close of World War I. At that time, as was pointed out at the beginning of this book, it occupied, including its League of Nations mandates, approximately one-quarter of the earth's surface and had under its wing about one-quarter of the earth's population. It ranked as the greatest, the wealthiest, and the most powerful aggregation of territories ever assembled under one banner in history.

If one considers the defeat of the Armada in 1588 as its birth date, it was a little less than three and a half centuries old. It had not taken shape according to any deliberate grand design, beginning rather with the quest of a diminutive and modestly wealthy island country for overseas trading facilities. Only later—from the seeds of political and economic understanding planted by such men as Raleigh with their insights into the values of foreign holdings; from the acquisitive work of such men as India's Robert Clive; and even as a result of the views of such men as Rudyard Kipling, with their Victorian ideas of the "white man's burden"—came the concept of Empire which held that a nation's prestige was enhanced, its military and political power strengthened, its people given a greater mobility, its social responsibilities more fully met, and its economy broadened by overseas possessions that were something more than trading stations, that were, in fact, extensions of the homeland.

The growth of Empire had taken place in two stages in the eras of the First and Second Empires: the first running from the Armada to the loss of the American colonies, and the second from the winning of Canada to the young manhood of the present century. Now, with World War I settled, that second stage was about to end. In fact, the idea of Empire itself was about to end.

To say that the British Empire was about to fall or die has a poetic and dramatic ring to it. It is not, however, the precise truth. The age of Empire was to pass, yes, and many of the lands that Britain had so long held were to slip from its grasp. But the geographic, political, and social amalgamation that was Empire was not to die. Though reduced mightily in size, it was still to encompass a staggering total of square miles. And though altered politically and socially, it was still to have at its core a strong sense of common loyalties among its member states and a healthy understanding on their part of the mutual advantages in the association.

Rather, the amalgamation was to change in essence. It was to transform itself from an Empire to a group of states in which each member state was equal to the other. The new arrangement was to be called, first, the British Commonwealth of Nations and then, some years later, simply the Commonwealth of Nations.

Many political, social, and economic factors had played a part in the building of the Empire. Now, several similar factors were to create the tapestry of Commonwealth that replaced it.

First, there was the liberal viewpoint found in many London quarters. It had been a strong force since the earliest days of colonization and had always called for some degree of self-rule for the overseas possessions. At times, particularly in the case of Lord Durham and Canada, it had even advised complete self-rule. A force that had never been totally extinguished, not even in the times of harshest Crown and parliamentary rule, it was now stronger than ever before, with an increasing number of Britishers feeling that political independence was a natural right of man and that the peoples of the overseas holdings were entitled to hold it.

Next, there was the growing economic and political strength of many of the holdings. The stronger that they became, the less willing were they to remain tied to the mother country. They wanted to try life on their own.

Finally, there was in this century a flowering of a sense of national identity and purpose in many of the Empire's possessions. They wanted to build their own governments and have their own people run them. They wanted the respect that came with being independent nations. They

wanted to pursue their own destinies. They no longer
wanted to be the children, or the vassals, of a distant mother
country.

This nationalism is one of the hallmarks of our century.
It has been, and continues to be, a driving force in contem-
porary history, rearranging the political structures of many
states, prompting the abandonment of old ties, and thrusting
upon many states the awesome responsibilities and disci-
plines of independence before they were ready for them.
In the case of the British Empire, it has been a force too
powerful and too inviting to be ignored or turned aside by
either the possessor or the possessed. It has been seen most
vividly in those Empire areas that were, or thought themselves to be, the most oppressed, or the least free. Chief
among their number have been Ireland, India, and the various lands of Africa. It is principally with their histories that
we will tell the story of the transformation from Empire to
Commonwealth.

Ever since 1170, when England's Henry II had sent troops
into Ireland to restore the rebel-deposed Dermot McMur-
rough to the throne of his Dublin kingdom and then, as
payment for the enterprise, had declared himself "Lord of
Ireland," the island nation had been one of Britain's most
cantankerous holdings and, most often, with valid reason.

The seed of the problem—and its most enduring aspect,
as is demonstrated by today's tragic events in Northern
Ireland—is to be found in the Protestant-Catholic enmities
created by the English monarchs of the fifteenth to seventeenth centuries. When Henry II made himself "Lord of

Ireland," his jurisdiction applied to just one kingdom in what at the time was a five-kingdom nation, but two later Henrys—Henry VII and Henry VIII—forcibly extended English rule to the rest of the island, with the latter especially infuriating the Irish. Naming himself "King of Ireland," he set about wiping out Catholicism in a country whose population was four-fifths Catholic, and replacing it with his own Church of England. To that end, he closed all the island's monasteries, which for centuries had been acknowledged throughout Europe as among the foremost centers of western culture and education. Next, Elizabeth continued and intensified his efforts, suppressing Catholicism wherever she found it. She ordered all Catholic services to be discontinued and took to herself the sole responsibility for appointing Irish bishops. When the Irish rebelled at her tactics, she reacted so violently and sent troops into the island with such repressive instructions that the country was left almost in ruins at the close of her reign.

Historian Seumas MacManus tells us how hard her hand fell. He writes that her government enacted laws which called for every Catholic priest found in Ireland after a certain date to be considered guilty of rebellion. He was to be hanged; his head was to be taken off and fixed on a pole in a public place; and his bowels were to be removed and burned.

MacManus adds that a Bishop Patrick O'Healy and a Cornelius Ryan were put to the rack. Their hands and feet were broken by hammers, and needles were pushed up under their nails. They were finally hanged and quartered. Also in Elizabeth's time, he continues, the price set for the

capture of a priest was the same as that for a wolf. (Mac-
Manus, in a footnote, names the usual price as five pounds,
but mentions a member of Parliament who was willing to
see the rate jump to ten pounds.) Further, the law of Recu-
sancy was passed. It established penalties for all who refused to attend services in the new religion.

To point up further the horrors of Irish life under Elizabeth, MacManus quotes the noted nineteenth-century Irish
historian, William Edward Lecky, who remarked that the
killing of Irishmen was seen as the killing of wild beasts.[19]

MacManus's writing leaves little doubt that the terrors of
an early religious persecution were such as to set a tradition
of bitter Irish enmity that would survive even into our own
time. Elizabeth incurred additional Irish wrath by pirating
great chunks of agricultural land and handing them over to
the British aristocracy for development as feudal estates, or,
as she called them, "plantations"; the practice saw their former owners and renters turned into tenant farmers for their
new overlords. After Elizabeth, James I continued the campaign to wipe out Catholicism by installing Scotch Protestant settlers in the northern reaches of the island.

The suppression continued throughout the seventeenth
and eighteenth centuries, with Catholics being refused seats
in the Irish parliament, and with the British lashing out in
other directions, some cultural, some economic. English replaced Gaelic as the country's official language; instilled in
the Irish was the same fear that was beginning to show itself
in the people of India and that would later rank high among
the factors driving the Boers to abandon Africa's Cape Colony; in the loss of their language and all the ancient history

and heritage that went with it, they saw their cultural annihilation. The pirating of land for "plantations" remained in vogue, with its hard practice of summarily evicting tenant farmers who failed in their rent payments; as did the land transfer and tax measures in India, the plantation system ruined the island's agrarian economy. And the passage of the Navigation Acts, which aroused so much American colonial wrath, severely curtailed what had been a flourishing Irish trade with continental Europe since the fourteenth century. Further, the acts were later amended to prohibit Irish use of ships that were not built in England and were not mastered by British skippers and manned three-quarters by British crews. MacManus says that the amendment all but wiped out the country's continental trade and, though it did wonders for British maritime interests, completely destroyed the Irish ship-building industry.[20]

If Ireland saw the British as cruel overseers, stamping out her religion and language, subjugating her people, and destroying her economy for the sake of their own pocketbooks, then the British saw Ireland as the most tempestuous of their holdings, always requiring harsh measures—sometimes the harshest—to keep her at heel. And tempestuous she was; there can be no arguing that point. Rebellion, so the British thought, seemed the word best understood and most cherished by her people.

The Irish had instituted their tradition of rebellion in the sixteenth century when they had risen against Elizabeth's religious oppressions and land grabs. An Irish chieftain, Shane O'Neill, had started things off with a string of unsuccessful outbreaks in 1567 and had been followed by his cousin, Hugh O'Neill, and the Earl of Desmond, both of whom inspired revolutions that were finally smashed at the opening of the seventeenth century. Rebellions continued to be the order of the day throughout the 1600s, all of them being efficiently crushed. Next, in the closing two years of the eighteenth century, the Irish—led by Theobald Wolfe Tone, a Protestant of English descent who, nevertheless, wanted to see the country free of Crown rule—schemed with the French to oust the British and replace them with a republican form of government. The revolt resulted in months of vicious fighting and acts of atrocity and brutality committed by both sides. In all, it netted the island nothing but the sacrifice of much blood and the loss of yet another privilege—internal self-government.

Hitherto, Ireland had been allowed to govern her internal affairs with her own parliament. It was, in the eyes of most Irishmen, not any sort of representative body for the country, what with Catholics being forbidden membership in it, but it was, at the least, better than no Irish parliament at all, and now it was taken away. In the Act of Union, which took effect in 1800, both the London parliament and the Irish parliament (whose Anglican membership was, of course, in sympathy with British rule) abolished the latter and passed the responsibility for making all Irish laws to the London body. Created by the act was the United Kingdom of Great Britain and Ireland, tying the two islands firmly together, with one subservient to the other. Ireland was granted a number of seats in the London parliament, but she was seldom able to muster the support necessary to pass legislation pleasing or favorable to her. Angrily, Ireland's people responded with a series of minor but vicious uprisings that were just as viciously quashed.

Oddly enough, though the nineteenth century got off to a poor start, it was marked by several political accomplishments that relieved somewhat Britain's stranglehold on the vassal nation. They were principally the work of two statesmen—one an Irishman, the other an Englishman—and they were hallmarks of a changing outlook, presages of an era of liberal political attitude. Just as the age of scientific appreciation was dawning, so was the age of democratic thought. So far as Ireland was concerned, the new era was best reflected in Irishman Daniel O'Connell and Englishman William Gladstone, both superb statesmen.

In the early 1800s, O'Connell, a lawyer who became known to his people as "the Liberator," formed an association of Irish Catholics for the purpose of winning political rights for them. Charging membership dues of only a penny a month, he attracted countless laborers and poor farmers to the organization's ranks. With the soon massive association behind him, O'Connell developed into such a powerful political force that he was able to have Parliament enact the Catholic Emancipation Act in 1829. It ended the long practice of denying Catholics the right to hold public office and to seek parliamentary seats.

Gladstone's greatest work on Ireland's behalf was accomplished in the final decades of the 1800s while he was serving as Britain's prime minister. An Englishman who had long been outraged by his nation's Irish practices, he brought about the disestablishment of the Church of England there, freeing the Irish of the awful burden of paying taxes to support it. Next, he fought for and achieved a series of land reforms. Hitherto, British landlords had been free to evict tenant farmers if rents went unpaid; now, Gladstone made eviction far less appealing by the passage of a law requiring a landlord to pay for any improvements made by the tenant prior to eviction. In another move, he led the British government to establish a fund of one million pounds to help tenants buy farms of their own at a cost usually well below the rents they had paid.

But the century was also one in which disaster visited Ireland. Between 1845 and 1848, a blight of unknown origin struck the island's potato crop, causing famine throughout the land. At the time, the crop was as vital to Ireland as rice was to Asia, for about half the population operated small farms and fed their families principally on potatoes, while the great percentage who worked as tenant farmers had only potatoes left for themselves after they had sold their grain and livestock to pay their rents. To make matters worse, there was an epidemic of typhus at the same time and, between illness and starvation, some 750,000 deaths were recorded between 1845 and 1847. The British shipped in tons of soup and cornmeal, but could not stem the tragic tide. The famine forced countless Irishmen to flee the country and seek a livelihood elsewhere, with most of their number going to the United States. It marked the start of an exodus that continued into the twentieth century, dropping the country's population from 8,250,000 in 1846 to 4,200,000 in 1921.

Though O'Connell had done much to emancipate the Catholics and Gladstone had bettered the lot of tenant farmers, one over-riding problem remained throughout the closing decades of the nineteenth century. The Irish wanted political independence and the rebirth of the Irish parliament. This is not to say that they were, at the time, desirous of a complete break with Britain. The present generations had been brought up under Crown rule and, despite the difficulties of the past, were content to remain within the framework of Empire; thousands, as is true of so many people everywhere, were too mild-mannered and too busy trying to earn a living to want the upheaval that would accompany any quest for total independence; others were content with the improvements wrought by O'Connell and Gladstone; and many, especially the Protestant population that had first been installed in Northern Ireland by James I, were quite loyal to the Crown. And, finally, the sense of nationalism that had fired earlier rebellions and that would fire the great outbreak of the early twentieth century seemed to be dormant. What the Irish wanted was what they called "Home Rule," an arrangement by which they could govern their own affairs and still remain within the Empire.

The drive toward Home Rule was begun in 1871 by Isaac Butt, a Dublin barrister. On his death in 1879, it was continued by Charles Stewart Parnell, a Protestant landlord who detested Ireland's vassalage to Britain. A dedicated fighter and a talented leader, he immediately caught the sympathetic eye of Gladstone when he entered Parliament in the 1870s. Aligning himself with Parnell, Gladstone in 1886 introduced the first of what were to be three Home Rule bills, all calling for the re-establishment of the Irish parliament. The bill was defeated. A second bill was introduced in 1893, two years after Parnell's death, and, though it passed in the House of Commons, it was struck down in the House of Lords, after which Gladstone retired as prime minister. The third and final Home Rule bill, backed by Prime Minister Herbert Asquith, was approved by Parliament in 1914. Passage of the bill marked a great triumph for the democratic spirit that had been spreading through Britain for more than a century, but the provisions of the bill were not destined to take immediate effect. In the years of its passage, World War I erupted, and the decision was made not to render it operative until the close of hostilities. That decision set the stage for the Irish uprising which culminated in independence for all of Ireland, except for six northern counties.

Before that uprising can be described, a change must be discussed that occurred in the spirit of many of the Irish as the nineteenth century dissolved into the twentieth. It was a change that summoned up a rebirth of Irish nationalism, a new interest in and appreciation for ancient Irish history and literature, a new desire to speak and preserve the Gaelic tongue, a new pride in the revolutionary heroes of old, and an intensification of the yearning for independence—most often, the yearning for *complete* independence, complete freedom from Britain. The change was most visibly seen in a series of organizations that sprang up throughout the southern regions of the country. These were such groups as the Gaelic League, dedicated to the revitalization of the love for the Gaelic language and the literature of the nation; the Gaelic Athletic Association, the Dungannon Clubs, the Irish Republican Brotherhood, the Irish Republican Army, and the Sinn Fein (*Ourselves Alone*) political party, all firmly determined to oust the British, some wanting to see the job done through peaceable political action, others of a more militant ilk willing to see it done with spilled blood.

Still another organization of the day was the Irish Volunteers, a civilian army headed by a schoolteacher-poet named Padraic Pearse and a professor of history at Dublin's Catholic University, Eoin MacNeill. It was formed in late 1913 to serve as a counterbalance to a Northern Ireland unit called the Ulster Volunteers. The Ulster force—vociferous, militant, and intensely loyal to the Crown—was attempting to sabotage the upcoming 1914 Home Rule bill by threatening trouble if it were passed, and Pearse and MacNeill hoped that the presence of the pro-Home Rule Irish Volunteers in the South might weaken the impact of the threats.

MacNeill hoped that freedom from Britain could be eventually realized without bloodshed. But, in the next few months, the ranks of his Volunteers were heavily infiltrated by members of the highly militant Irish Republican Brotherhood. They were outraged when implementation of the 1914 Home Rule Act was postponed by World War I. Further, they feared that Irishmen would be conscripted into the British army and made to fight for their hated overlord. Both these factors drove them to plot a revolution in 1916 in which Pearse—himself a militant and a man possessed of the poetic notion that revolution and spilled blood would somehow "purify" the long-enslaved Irish spirit—willingly joined.

The rebellion was planned for Easter Sunday, 1916, and was kept a secret from MacNeill, on the valid grounds that

he would certainly object to the violence and would consider the whole enterprise, which had to face superior British forces, doomed from the start. The plan called for the
trouble to break out in Dublin and its outlying areas, the
hope being that it would kindle uprisings throughout the
rest of the country. But, on the eve of hostilities, MacNeill
caught wind of the scheme, was predictably horrified, and
took steps to halt it, sending out orders to the leaders of all
Volunteer units to keep their men at home. The instructions
were ignored in some quarters and countermanded in others. In the resulting confusion, the outbreak was delayed
one day and, when the Volunteers finally took to the streets
on Easter Monday, April 24, they mustered only 1,200 men
out of their total force of 16,000. Nevertheless, they immediately installed themselves—and threw up barricades—in
several strategic locations, among them the General Post
Office in the heart of the city. From its front steps, after the
Union Jack had been hauled down, Padraic Pearse read a
statement proclaiming Ireland an independent republic.
Within hours, fighting was underway that was to last until
late the following Saturday afternoon.

A group of young Volunteers got things started by attacking a British ammunition dump on Dublin's outskirts
and blowing up a part of its stores. A small troop stormed
the gates of Dublin Castle, for centuries the seat of the British authority in Ireland, but fell back minutes later, thinking
it more heavily fortified than it was; actually, there were
just a few men inside and it could have fallen easily into
Irish hands and become a mighty symbol of revolutionary
victory for the entire country. A troop of British lancers

marched on the General Post Office. Pearse's men, barricaded behind furniture and sandbags, opened fire and
dropped the lancer commander in his tracks. His troopers,
taken by surprise and now leaderless, retreated. The encounter was to be one of the last Volunteer victories in the
revolt.

The hoped-for nationwide uprisings failed to materialize,
and in the next few days British might began to close in on
Dublin. First came a contingent of 3,700 troops from their
barracks outside the city. Then from across the Irish Sea
came British cannon, machine guns, and heavy reinforcements. By Thursday, Dublin was completely ringed and
the Britishers were tightening the circle, methodically chok-
ing off one rebel post after another as they advanced. By
Friday, only the General Post Office had not fallen into their
hands.

Throughout Friday night and most of Saturday, British
artillery reduced the building to a blazing shell. The Volunteers, firing from upper story windows, kept the attacking
infantry at bay, but Pearse knew that the cause was lost,
that it was only a matter of time before the fortification had
to be abandoned. For a while, he debated sending his men
into the street to take up positions elsewhere, but finally
rejected the idea; it would only result in every Volunteer
being shot down as he dashed from the building. At 3:45
P.M., Saturday, April 29, he walked slowly outside and surrendered.

The Easter Uprising, as it came to be called, was at an
end, a total failure. But, in its wake, there erupted throughout Ireland the very outbreaks that had been so hoped for

during the long week of fighting. Causing the outbreaks were three British blunders, two of them outrageous.

The first was committed by General Sir John Maxwell, the commanding officer of the British forces in Ireland. At the close of the Easter Uprising, he was not content simply to accept a surrender. Rather, he was determined to break the revolutionary spirit and terrify the people so they would never make trouble again. With this purpose in mind, he imprisoned Pearse and thirteen other Volunteer leaders, sentenced them to death without open trials, and, over a period of two weeks, had them executed. Hitherto, the independence movement had been supported by relatively few of the Irish population, principally those of an intellectual or radical bent. But now, thanks to Maxwell's brutality, fury spread throughout Ireland's southern regions. Pearse and his fellow leaders became national heroes, martyrs to the cause of freedom. More than had ever been the case in recent years, the island country was ripe for wholesale rebellion.

The second blunder was made in late 1917 when British Prime Minister Lloyd George, just eighteen months after the Easter Uprising, called a meeting with Irish leaders to discuss implementation of the long-delayed Home Rule Act. Lloyd George had two reasons for wanting the session, which became known as the Irish Convention. First, he was alarmed at the mounting unrest in the south of the island. Second, he was keeping close tabs on the attitude of the Irish living in the United States. They were vocally indignant over the events following the Uprising, and Lloyd George was concerned that they might give rise to such a wave of anti-British sentiment across the Atlantic that America's impending entry into World War I might be delayed or sidetracked altogether. The idea for the convention, holding out the possibility of quieting both Ireland and the United States, was a sound one, but it was destroyed by an ill-timed British move quite outside its confines. During the first three years of war, Irish enlistment in the British army had been on a voluntary basis, and conscription, though often discussed, had never been enacted. Now, just as the convention went into session, London instituted Irish conscription. The result: a fresh wave of indignation, with the Irish calling it sheer hypocrisy for Lloyd George to be chatting about Home Rule at the very time his government was authorizing a draft.

The British committed their third blunder by blaming the Easter Uprising not only on the Volunteers but also on the Sinn Fein political party, which actually had nothing to do with its plotting aside from the fact that a number of Volunteers were coincidentally Sinn Feiners. Prior to the rebellion, the party had been growing slowly. Now—with some knowing the truth and resenting the charge, and with others suddenly sympathetic to the party because they believed the accusation—the freshly angered Irish people gave the Sinn Fein increasing support. Consequently, seventy-three Sinn Feiners were elected to Parliament in 1918, giving the party its largest representation there to date.

Those seventy-three men set the stage for the next period of open warfare on the island. They did so by refusing to go to London. Instead, they gathered in Dublin, created the Dail Eireann (Chamber of Deputies), declared Ireland a republic on January 21, 1919, and established a provisional government, naming Eamon de Valera its president. American-born, the son of a Spanish father and an Irish mother, de Valera had helped to plot the Uprising and had been the only Volunteer leader to escape execution, which, a number of Irish suspected, might have been accounted for by his American birth; even Maxwell would have been sensitive to United States wrath. The British attempted to suppress the infant government, with the result that the party's military branch—the Irish Republican Army—took up arms. There followed a struggle of more than two years that the British called the Anglo-Irish War and that the Irish simply christened "The Troubles."

Leading the I.R.A. was Michael Collins, a one-time postal clerk and former member of the Volunteers. Knowing that his forces would be doomed if ever they met the better-equipped and trained British in open battle, he decided on a guerrilla type of fighting that was intended to drive the enemy out by reducing their daily activities to chaos. Accordingly, he ordered that British truck transports be attacked, that British patrols be ambushed, that sentries be murdered at their posts, that railway lines be destroyed, and that British garrisons and storage depots be bombed.

For their part, the British reinforced their garrisons with regular troops and strengthened the ranks of the police with a force of unemployed World War I veterans who—because of their black-coated and tan-trousered uniforms—were soon known as the "Black and Tans." And, just as soon, they were the most hated men in Ireland. They responded to Collins's guerrilla tactics with a reign of terror of their own, inspired in great part by fear of the I.R.A.'s ruthlessness. They tracked down or ambushed I.R.A. men wherever they could find them, sometimes killing innocent citizens in the process. They broke into homes and public places in search of revolutionaries. They tortured prisoners for information. At times abandoning their uniforms and disguising themselves in civilian clothes, they trapped un- suspecting I.R.A. troopers and shot them down or roughly took them prisoners.

The atrocities committed on both sides aroused shocked outcries in Ireland and Britain and among the Irish popu- lation in the United States. The demand that the killing be stopped mounted until, in 1921, Prime Minister Lloyd George and his cabinet could no longer ignore it. In July of that year, they began a series of peace talks with Sinn Fein officials, Collins among them. The talks lasted for five months and ended on December 6 with the signing of a treaty that established the Irish Free State—in Gaelic, *Saorstát Éireann*—and granted it dominion status within the Empire.

The Sinn Fein representatives came to the talks wanting complete freedom from Britain, but, thanks to some hard bargaining on Llyod George's part, agreed to the Free State concept and the self-government that it promised. They agreed, too, that Ireland's six northern counties should be left out of the State, for their people were predominantly Protestant and did not wish to associate themselves politi- cally with the principally Catholic population to the south. Accordingly, the 1801 designation of the United Kingdom of Great Britain and Ireland was revised to the United King- dom of Great Britain and Northern Ireland.

But no sooner had the Irish Free State been formed and

dominion status achieved than there was trouble within the
ranks of the Sinn Fein. At the core of the difficulty was
de Valera. He still wanted to see a complete break with
Britain, and, just as fiercely, he wanted a united Ireland,
one that embraced both the southern and northern regions
of the country. Between late 1921 and early 1923, civil war
raged between his followers and those Sinn Feiners agree-
able to the Free State arrangement. Peace was finally restored so that the killing could be stopped, but de Valera,
with his goals still unrealized, then split the party into factions. One (the Fianna Fail) was headed by himself and
was manned by his supporters. William T. Cosgrove took
over the other faction and led the Free State government
throughout the remainder of the 1920s and earned for himself the reputation of an able statesman, rebuilding the
nation's economy and establishing strong and profitable
trade relations with Britain.

De Valera remained out of the government for the next
four years, persistently championing the idea of a united
Ireland and disassociation from Britain. However, when
he saw that his position was losing some favor in the light
of Cosgrove's economic improvements, he realized that he
could never free the country from Empire unless he held
an official post of high order. Consequently, he returned to
government in 1927 and won for himself and many of his
supporters election to the Dail Eireann. In 1933, he replaced
Cosgrove as the president of the Executive Council, the
body that governed the State. Once in office, he began a
program to break the ties with Britain, a program that was
to be completed in 1949 by another Irish leader.

First, de Valera did away with the oath of allegiance to the

British Crown that the State had been made to declare upon its formation. Next, he abolished the post of the British governor-general, a position that had come into being shortly after the State's organization. Then, in 1937, he led the Dail Eireann in framing a new constitution for the country and in replacing the State's name with a new one—*Éire,* Ireland's ancient name in Gaelic. With its new constitution, Ireland declared itself a sovereign nation, but one that—because its economy and resources were not yet fully ready for complete self-sufficiency—retained an allegiance to Britain. The constitution called for a president and a prime minister. De Valera was named to the latter post, and an Irish scholar, Douglas Hyde, assumed the presidency.

Complete independence did not come for another twelve years, at which time de Valera was not in power. The final break took place in 1949, when he had been out of office for several months.* On April 18 of that year, the recently named Prime Minister John A. Costello declared Ireland a republic (a declaration that was recognized in Britain in the next months) which, free and independent of Britain, withdrew from the Commonwealth of Nations.

By the time that Ireland declared itself a republic in 1949, the idea of a British Empire had been dead for eighteen years and had been replaced by the concept of Commonwealth. The transformation from Empire to Commonwealth had been accomplished in 1931 and had been made possible by the Statute of Westminster.

---

* De Valera returned as prime minister in 1951 and 1957, resigning in 1959 to become president of Ireland.

The change, however, did not take place overnight. It was, rather, a process of evolution that could be traced back to the late nineteenth century and the inauguration of what were called Imperial Conferences. They were meetings that, held periodically throughout the coming years, brought the heads of state in the dominions together with representatives of the London government to discuss such matters as Empire and individual problems, Empire and individual policies, and the needs of common defense.

In the beginning, Britain sat as the chief power at the conferences, as indeed she was. She was the mother country, strong through the oath of allegiance that each dominion had sworn to the Crown at the time of its formation. And, though the dominions held the right of independent internal rule, she retained the responsibility for setting foreign policy for the Empire, policy that had an effect on them all. Also, though they had the privilege of internal rule, she was permitted by such statutes as the Colonial Acts Validity Laws to intervene in any dominion's legislation that she thought unwise for or damaging to the Empire as a whole.

But, as the meetings moved into the twentieth century, the growing power of the dominions became manifest. Jan Christiaan Smuts of the Union of South Africa and Prime Minister Robert Borden of Canada, for example, were awarded seats in the Imperial War Cabinet during World War I and had strong voices in the determination and direction of the Empire's foreign policies. Then, at the Paris Peace Conference that followed the war, each dominion was given separate representation. Their support of the mother country's foreign dealings was traditionally requested, but not demanded, and they considered the requests with increasing caution, weighing them in the light of their own growing individual interests and responsibilities. A case in point is the Locarno Treaties of 1925, in which Britain, France, Germany, Belgium, and Italy reached a series of post-war agreements, in particular a number resolving border questions; it was left up to each dominion to decide whether it wished to go along with the responsibilities that Britain assumed with her plans for maintaining international peace. Further, just two years earlier, each dominion had won the right to negotiate and sign on its own any treaties that directly affected it.

Britain saw the growing dominion power and wisely bent herself to it, prompted by her own democratic beliefs and having the good sense to realize that resistance would only cause trouble; besides, she realized that resistance would be fruitless, for independence was the rising and irresistible tide not only of the present but of the future. In the mid-1920s, she acknowledged the growing status of the dominions by placing their dealings with the mother country in a special office. Until then, such dealings had been in the care of the Colonial Office, the bureau responsible for administering the relations with all Empire holdings. Now the dominions were given a department of their own, handled by a secretary of state for dominion affairs. Then the mother country began looking for a new governmental framework in which she and the dominions could better and more realistically function.

That framework proved to be the Commonwealth. It was a concept that was placed before the Imperial Conference of 1926 by British statesman Arthur Balfour speaking on behalf of the homeland government. In his presentation, Balfour defined the dominions as "autonomous communities within the British Empire, equal in status, in no way subordinate one to another in any aspect of their domestic or external affairs, though united by a common allegiance to the Crown and freely associated as members in the British Commonwealth of Nations." He went on to say that, according to this definition, Britain would no longer have the right granted to her by the old Colonial Acts Validity Laws to intervene in or disallow dominion legislation; from now on, Britain would be able to legislate for a dominion only at the dominion's request. Further, in respect to any dominion legislation, the Crown would be advised only by the dominion involved and not by the London government. Balfour added, however, that the responsibility for defense and foreign policy must "for some time to come" remain with Great Britain.[21]

The Balfour definition was taken under study during the next few years and the machinery necessary to make it legal and functional was established. The whole Commonwealth concept and its attendant machinery were then put on paper in what came to be called the Statute of Westminster. The Statute won Parliamentary approval in 1931.

With it, the dominions—Canada, Newfoundland (yet to be absorbed as a Canadian province), Australia, New Zealand, the Union of South Africa, and the Irish Free State—joined the United Kingdom as equal members in a world-wide family that was formally christened the British Commonwealth of Nations.

The transformation was complete. The era of Empire was at an end. Born was the age of Commonwealth.

Chapter Ten

Transition: India

WHEN THE COMMONWEALTH came into existence, most Empire holdings below dominion rank were left under Britain's wing, with a few, principally because of their locations, being granted to Australia and New Zealand as dependencies.* Of those remaining with Britain, the largest by far was that "brightest jewel," India. It is to her story that we now turn.

The history of India, from the very moment that the nation became British India and its supportive states, was to be one of even greater turbulence than before, marked by the incessant and invariably mounting call for independence. The independence agitation in India, Ireland, and the African regions, as well as the growing prestige of the dominions,

---

* See the table beginning on page 256.

accounted in no small part for Britain's realization that the Empire of old must be replaced by the more attractive and flexible Commonwealth plan. As a result, India achieved dominion status in 1947 and became an independent republic within the Commonwealth in 1950.

As noted earlier, when the British assumed control of India in 1858, their rule extended directly to approximately 60 percent of its land area and 80 percent of its population, with the heads of state of the remaining regions agreeing to support and cooperate with the new overlords. The directly ruled area became British India (the term Indian Empire was used to refer to the entire country). It was put in the administrative hands of a viceroy, and was divided into some fifteen provinces, each headed by a governor who was answerable to the viceroy. British rule itself, was, according to the Indians, the Raj, a shortening of their word rajah, meaning ruler.

No sooner were the new overlords in office than they heard the rumblings of discontent and the demand for independence. As in the days of the East India Company, many Indians felt that they were being exploited by the British. They complained that an outsider had relegated them to the role of servants, paying them poorly and looking down on them as racially inferior. Others resented the presence of British troops, claiming that the necessity of keeping them fed accounted for India's many famines—a charge that completely ignored a history of periodic famine predating the arrival of Europeans. Still others muttered that job opportunities in government service were denied them. In that charge there was solid truth, for the civil service of the day was manned principally by Britons and, though an Indian could apply for a position, he was required to make an impossibly expensive journey to London to sit for a pre-employment examination. And still others feared that the Raj was trying to wipe out their ancient culture with its system of English-speaking education. This complaint dated back to 1835 when Thomas Babington Macaulay, the renowned English historian-poet and one-time adviser on Indian affairs, had written what he titled his *Minute on Education* and had sold Britain on the idea of putting its concepts to use. In the *Minute*, Macaulay advised the use of the English language in Indian education and called for a system of Indian schools that would "form a class who may be interpreters between us and the millions whom we govern; a class of persons, Indian in blood and color, but English in taste, in opinions, in morals and intellect." [22]

Some historians have damned the *Minute* as a piece of unmitigated arrogance, charging that what Macaulay had in mind was an army of Indians who would be trained to serve the British and to do precisely whatever they were told. This view may or may not be true, but, in Macaulay's defense, it must be noted that he also wrote:

"It may be that the public mind of India may expand under our system till it has outgrown our system; that by good government we may educate our subjects into a capacity for better government; that, having become instructed in European knowledge they may, in some future age, demand European institutions. Whether such a day will ever come I know not. But never will I attempt to retard or avert it. Whenever it comes it will be the proudest day in English history." [23]

Whatever motives he may have had in mind, the institu-

tion of Macaulay's advice in India had three results: first, it
served to weld together a country whose traditional divisions
had always been caused in great part by its variety of languages; second, it provided a corps of educated Indians able
to use Western skills and assist the British in the expansion
of such needed facilities as railroads, better roadways, irrigation systems, and improved agricultural procedures; third—
and, so far as Raj was concerned, unfortunate—it developed
countless Indians into thinkers fired by Western ideas of
liberty and determined to apply them to their own country.

By the 1870s, these dissident Indians were making themselves heard: Indian newspapers were openly criticizing
British authority; writers and poets—as would Ireland's men
of letters in the dawning twentieth century—were producing
works that summoned up memories of pride in the wonders
of India's early civilizations and philosophies; scholars and
political figures were speaking of man's basic right to govern
his own life, to live free of the yoke of another.

In an attempt to quiet the many voices and lay their criti-
cisms to rest, Britain in 1885 approved the formation of the
Indian National Congress. As first proposed, the Congress
was intended to promote understanding between the Indian
peoples and the Raj. Indeed, with representatives from all
parts of India and from the nation's various religions and
castes joining it, it did for a time serve that very purpose. But,
in time, such eloquent advocates of independence as politi-
cian Bal Gangaghar Tilak and poet Rabindranath Tagore
became important figures in the Congress and it began to
concern itself almost entirely with the wholesale broadcast-
ing of Indian grievances, thus disappointing and angering
the British.

The grievances erupted into open violence in the twentieth century when Lord Curzon (George Nathaniel Curzon), who served as viceroy from 1899 to 1905, partitioned the great Bengal region into two separate provinces for the sake of a more efficient administration. Actually, the move was a sound one, for the area was far too sprawling to be effectively supervised from a single headquarters. But Curzon's action outraged Bengal's 80 million people, all of whom looked on their homeland as sacred. Rioting broke out at Calcutta and elsewhere. British buildings were bombed and government representatives attacked. So bad did the situation become that the partition decision was reversed and Lord Curzon was removed from office. (In fairness, it must be noted that Lord Curzon, otherwise an extremely capable administrator, was not removed because of the partition problem alone; also accounting for his dismissal were political disagreements with a number of reigning British officials in India, among them the army's Lord Kitchener.)

In addition to the cancellation of the partition, the violence won for the Indians several political rewards. They came in 1909, in the Indian Councils Act (otherwise known as the Morley-Minto reforms for their authors, John Morley and Gilbert Minto) and marked one of the first steps toward the nation's eventual self-government. At the time, each province was administered not only by a governor but by a legislative council, and the Act enabled Indians for the first time to be elected to council seats. Further, the viceroy was counseled in his decisions by an advisory council; the Act now called for one of its members to be an Indian.

Thanks to the Act and to other measures—among them

the growing practice of admitting more Indians to the civil service—the political scene was quiet at the outbreak of World War I and the nation gave its support to the mother country, contributing some 1,401,000 men to the struggle. The support was even more willingly given when, in 1917, Britain promised that, as a reward, the end of hostilities would see her exert efforts for "the gradual development of self-governing institutions with a view to the progressive realization of responsible government in India as an integral part of the British Empire . . ." [24.]

It was a promise difficult to keep following so quickly a struggle that left Europe in chaos. When post-war reforms failed to take shape quickly, the Indians turned sullen and restive. Demonstrations, mass rallies, and riots broke out on a scale sufficient to cause the British to impose restrictions on Indian civil liberties. Among the restrictions were a ban on public meetings and a suspension of trial by jury.

The ban of public meetings resulted in the blackest incident of the period. On April 13, 1919, more than ten thousand Indians jammed themselves into a small park in the city of Amritsar to disobey and protest the ruling. When a detachment of British troops arrived to disperse the gathering, the officer in charge—the Indian-born Brigadier General Reginald Dyer, who believed in strict obedience to the Crown—ordered his men to fire into the crowd. In the next ten minutes of gunfire, as screaming Indians mobbed the park's single narrow exit in an attempt to escape, some 400 were killed and about 1,150 wounded.

The Amritsar Massacre, as it quickly came to be known, opened the door on a struggle for independence that continued unabated for almost two decades. So fierce now was the determination to be rid of the Raj that no conciliatory reforms could placate the Indians, including the measures of 1919 (the Montagu-Chelmsford reforms, named for their authors, Edwin S. Montagu and Lord Chelmsford, the former then secretary of state for India, the latter the viceroy) that awarded an increased degree of self-government to the provinces, upped the number of Indians on the viceroy's advisory council from one to three, and paved the way for greater Indian representation in the nation's central government. One Indian group after another was organized to give impetus to the independence movement, with all making themselves heard in demonstrations, rallies, and civil outbursts. The Indian National Congress accelerated its demands that the wartime promise of self-government be made good, that in keeping with the words "responsible government in India as an integral part of the British Empire" the country be awarded dominion status.

The chief figure to emerge in the movement at this time was a frail-looking lawyer with a deep and abiding compassion for society's downtrodden, Mohandas Karamchand Gandhi. With his strategy of non-violent disobedience against British authority, which was to be taken up later in other parts of the world by groups seeking political goals of their own, he welded the Indian people into an irresistible force for self-government.

Born in 1869 of a well-to-do and politically active family in western India, Gandhi took his law degree in London and practiced, not very successfully, for a brief period in his homeland. Then, in 1893, representing a Moslem com-

pany in a legal action, he went to South Africa and saw
the course of his life changed, for while there he was so
moved by the shameful treatment accorded Indians living
in Natal and the Transvaal that he determined to devote
all his energies to the struggle against social, economic, and
political discrimination. Back in India, preaching love for
all men and a reverence for all life, he added the independence movement to his dedications in the wake of the Amritsar Massacre. He attained the leadership of the Indian
National Congress in 1920 and persuaded that group to
adopt his strategy of non-violent disobedience, which he
called *"Satyagraha,"* or "soul force," from the Sanskrit word
that can be roughly translated as "steadfast grasping of
truth." The strategy not only dove-tailed with his philoso-
phy of gentleness and love toward all mankind, but also
struck him as the only way by which India could successfully deal with the British, avoiding as it would a direct
clash with their superior arms. It called for the people to
disrupt British activities by quietly lying in streets and on
railroad tracks to interfere with the flow of transport, block-
ing British shop entrances to halt business, and stretching
out in front of government buildings to upset the daily
work there. Further, and just as passively, Indians were
to ignore the payment of taxes, boycott English-speaking
schools, and refuse court appearances.

When first announced, the program immediately caught
the imagination of the man in the street. Then, once it was
adopted by the Indian National Congress, it extended itself
to the wealthier classes and soon won the support of some
of the country's most influential people. It became a mass

effort involving millions of Indians, that, for the simplest of reasons, completely frustrated the British. How could they successfully deal with an adversary who, when they moved to arrest him or to disperse his gatherings, greeted them with nothing more than a quiet smile?

In the 1930s the London government took steps to provide India with further self-government, which were intended to move her closer to dominion status. These steps were prompted not only by the restlessness of the Indian people but by the homeland's basically liberal viewpoint and its acknowledgment of the many Empire realities that had led to the 1931 Statute of Westminster. In 1935, Parliament approved the Government of India Act and created a new constitution for the nation. Increasing the autonomy of the provinces beyond the Montagu-Chelmsford reforms, it gave provincial legislatures (outgrowths of the original legislative councils) control over legislation in their areas. It permitted each governor to form a cabinet of members from the majority party in his province and provided that all cabinet members be Indians. It allowed the governors and the viceroy, however, to exercise a veto over legislation, and it left in the hands of the viceroy the administration of most of the country's finances.

With the coming of World War II, many Indians, despising the Axis, put aside their old animosities and threw their support behind the British. In time, the country housed many Allied air bases, produced a variety of military supplies, and sent troops to fight in the Middle East and France. But many other Indians, among them members of the Indian National Congress, refused their support. First, they plan, reverted to its old position, and declared August 16 as "Direct Action Day" to press its Pakistan demands. The activities of that day triggered weeks of rioting between Hindus and Moslems. Close to seven thousand Indians were killed in the outbreaks.

Britain herself brought the whole problem to an end in 1947 when Prime Minister Clement Attlee announced that his country would leave India by no later than June of the next year, regardless of whether the Congress and the League managed to get together and write a constitution. Viscount Louis Mountbatten, the newly appointed and last viceroy, met with the League and then the Congress, reporting to the latter the League's intention to revolt unless the independence included the establishing of Pakistan. Faced with the dilemma of the British departure on the one hand and the threat of nationwide bloodshed on the other, the Congress surrendered and reluctantly agreed to the formation of a state that would deprive India of approximately one-quarter of its land.

Immediately, an independence bill was drafted. It was enacted by Parliament in July of 1947 and took effect in the next month, creating two dominions—the Dominion of India on August 15, and the Dominion of Pakistan on the preceding day. Nehru became India's first prime minister, holding that position until his death in 1964. Jinnah, who was to die in 1948, was named governor-general of Pakistan; he was succeeded by Khwaja Nazimudden, who later became Pakistan's prime minister.

The creation of Pakistan left the Indian subcontinent in a turmoil. The new nation occupied two territories, separated from each other by approximately one thousand miles. The larger of the two lay in the northwest and arced northward along the borders of Iran and Afghanistan to the Indian state of Kashmir, now called Jammu and Kashmir. The second area lay in the northeast and occupied approximately half of the Bengal region. The Dominion of India covered the peninsula and extended up between the two Pakistan areas—which were soon being called East and West Pakistan—to its northern borders at the Himalayas. The immediate problem was the transfer of populations—Moslems from India to Pakistan, and Hindus from Pakistan to India. The shift caused weeks of terrible fighting between the two peoples, with riots, beatings, tortures, and murders becoming daily occurrences. One victim of the upheaval was Gandhi, who despaired of the fighting as a "spiritual tragedy" and a sad end to India's long struggle for independence. Irrationally, he became a figure hated by both sides, suffering the Moslem charge that he had obstructed the formation of Pakistan, and the Hindu accusation that he had supported it. On January 30, 1948, he fell victim to a Hindu assassin's bullet, dying moments later.

In the midst of the chaos, however, the Dominion of India took solid shape under Nehru's guidance. Upon independence, she immediately embraced the area of old British India, after which she entered into negotiations to absorb those states that had remained autonomous, but had nevertheless supported the Raj. Their rulers agreed to become part of the dominion in exchange for annual payments to them from the Indian government.

Then India took another major step. From the beginning,

lation—began clamoring for release from the British soon after World War II, wanting to unite themselves with Greece, which they considered the island's ancient homeland. Indeed, Cyprus had once been a Greek outpost, but had been held by the Turkish Ottoman Empire since the sixteenth century and had been seized by Britain in World War I. The demands for independence led to a civil war in the mid-1950s. Hostilities came to an end when Britain, Turkey, Greece, and Cyprus representatives met in 1959 and reached an agreement whereby the island would become an independent republic. Cyprus assumed its new status, and received Commonwealth membership, on August 16, 1960.

To the west, in the European area of the Mediterranean, the island of Malta, a Crown holding since British troops had ousted the French during the Napoleonic Wars, was peacefully granted its independence in 1964, joining the Commonwealth at that time. And to the west in the Indian Ocean, the 720-square-mile island of Mauritius, likewise a British possession since the days of Napoleon, became an independent nation and a Commonwealth member on March 12, 1968, functioning with a governor-general and a prime minister, and with the British Crown as head of state.

With but two exceptions, the growing tide of independence saw the Commonwealth gain as new members the departing holdings of Empire. The first of the two exceptions was to be found directly east of India—in Burma. Conquered by the British in three wars between 1824 and 1885, Burma was given internal self-government and a parliament in 1937. The Japanese invaded the country during

World War II and occupied it throughout, but, in some of the hardest fighting of the war, were driven out in the last days before peace was restored. Britain, acknowledging the coming independence of all Asia, immediately re-established the nation's parliament, urged the Burmese to write a constitution for an independent nation, and told them that they were free to decide whether they wished to join the Commonwealth. The country achieved its independence as the Union of Burma of January 4, 1948, and, in great measure due to the extremist factions within its borders, elected not to enter the Commonwealth.

The second exception was the ancient country of Palestine along the eastern shores of the Mediterranean. The British seized it from Turkish control during World War I, and, in 1923, were given it to administer as a League of Nations mandate, a mandate that continued until 1948. Throughout all the years between, the small land was the scene of a constant struggle between its Jewish and Arab populations.

The problem had begun late in the nineteenth century when the Zionist movement had been founded to establish Palestine as a homeland for Jews. It was a movement that saw several thousand Jews enter the country by World War I, much to the annoyance of the Arabs living there. In 1937, in an attempt to quiet the tensions, a British commission recommended that the country be partitioned into a state for Jews and a state for Arabs. The Arabs objected strongly, arguing that, instead, Palestine should be made into an independent state that recognized full minority rights for Jews. The British countered with the idea that, after a ten-year period of preparation, Palestine should be given an independence that would allow the Arabs and the Jews to share equal authority in government. The idea appealed to neither side, and Arab-Jewish friction intensified through the next years. The British mandate ended on May 14, 1948, and, with the question of independence still unsettled—and, consequently, with the question of Commonwealth membership never at stake—British forces withdrew from the country. Their departure brought on open Arab-Jewish fighting. Out of the conflict emerged the Republic of Israel.

In the stories of India, its surrounding Asian regions, Ireland, and the Statute of Westminster, we have traced the passing of Empire and the birth of Commonwealth. Now we come to Africa. Here, just as vividly, we shall see at work the very same forces of nationalism that spurred India and southern Ireland to independence. We shall see a mighty growth in the Commonwealth, with one emerging African nation after the other seeking and being granted membership in it. And, here, as in Burma and Palestine, we shall see the Commonwealth suffer losses.

Chapter Eleven

Transformation: Africa

WE BEGIN AT the southern tip of the continent.

From its formation following the Boer War, the Union of South Africa was split into two sharply opposed political factions, one willing to support Britain, the other persistent in its opposition to the mother country.

The conflict was most sharply defined in World Wars I and II when the nation threw in its lot with Britain, but did so in the face of strong protest by those who saw in a German victory the chance to oust the British and transform the country into an independent republic.

Greatly responsible for maintaining the ties with Britain was that one-time foe, the influential Jan Christiaan Smuts, who headed the country's United Party. In 1948, however, his party was defeated by its chief opponent, the National Party. With a heavy membership of Afrikaners, the Nationalists immediately pushed a program of *apartheid,* which, according to its definition, called for the separation of the black and white races. Apartheid leveled such strong repressive measures against the native Africans that it earned the condemnations of other Commonwealth nations and caused India, in 1954, to break off all relations with the Union because of the treatment given Indian minorities living there.

In 1959, the National Party, angered by the criticism from some of the Commonwealth nations and traditionally eager to be rid of any British affiliations, began planning a withdrawal from the Commonwealth, which was approved in a referendum of 1960. The Union of South Africa, on May 31, 1961, declared itself a republic and severed its Commonwealth ties.

Since that time, the Union's repressive racial policies have intensified. Native strikes and riots against the government in 1960 resulted in many deaths and imprisonments. In 1963, restrictions on the personal freedoms of black Africans were instituted. The United Nations, in 1966, terminated the country's mandate over South-West Africa because of its apartheid practices. The Union, which had held the mandate since the close of World War I, ignored the ruling and has continued to administer the region illegally ever since. In 1971, it offered to hold an election in which the people of South-West Africa could determine whether they wished South African or United Nations administration. The U.N. turned the offer down, saying that it had no validity because it came from an occupying power.

Now, what of the three regions—Bechuanaland, Basutoland, and Swaziland—that were allowed to remain outside the confines of the Union when it was formed in 1910? All remained in British care until the 1960s, each being given an increasing share of internal self-rule as time went on, and each, when independence came, being welcomed into the Commonwealth. Bechuanaland became the Republic of Botswana in 1965, four years after she had drafted her first constitution. Basutoland, renamed Lesotho, achieved the status of an independent kingdom on October 4, 1966. And on September 6, 1968, Swaziland was likewise declared an independent kingdom, with the ranking chief of its native tribes serving as its monarch, as he had since a 1941 Anglo-tribal agreement.

Moving now to the east—to the Rhodesias, Nyasaland, Tanganyika, Zanzibar, Kenya, Uganda, and Somaliland—we encounter a similar pattern: a series of Commonwealth gains and losses.

Just as apartheid led to the South African break with the Commonwealth so did it account for the 1965 departure of Rhodesia, formerly Southern Rhodesia.

In the late nineteenth century, as indicated in Chapter Eight, the vast area north of the Transvaal was first developed by Cecil Rhodes's South Africa Company and then divided into two regions—Southern Rhodesia (containing a larger population of Europeans) and Northern Rhodesia—with the British agreeing that the two should be administered by the company. In 1921, Southern Rhodesia broke away from the company, voted self-government for itself, and won the status of a self-governing colony. Northern Rhodesia remained with the company for another three

years, after which the country's administration was passed
to Britain.

In 1935, Britain united the Rhodesias with the neighboring territory of Nyasaland, a region that was principally
occupied by African tribes and that had been a British protectorate since 1892 as a safeguard against the intrusions of
Arab slavers. Together, the trio became the self-governing
Federation of Rhodesia and Nyasaland. The association was
never pleasing to the Africans of Nyasaland because of
Southern Rhodesia's growing apartheid policies. It was dissolved in 1964, with its members going their separate ways.
In the year of the break-up—on July 6—Nyasaland became
the independent nation of Malawi. Two years later, again
on July 6, it emerged as a republic. For its part, Northern
Rhodesia changed its name to Zambia and established itself
as a republic on October 24, 1964. Both infant nations entered the Commonwealth.

So much for the first gains. Now for a loss.

Southern Rhodesia had found its relations with Britain
growing increasingly strained during the eleven years of
the Federation, thanks to the country's apartheid practices,
which closely equaled those of South Africa in their repres-
siveness. In 1964, with the Federation dissolving, Southern
Rhodesia demanded independence from Britain, a demand
that the British would not grant until guaranteed that the
Africans there would be given a solid voice in government. Furious, Southern Rhodesia, led by Prime Minister
Ian Smith and now calling itself simply Rhodesia, declared
itself an independent nation on November 11, 1965, free of
Britain and the Commonwealth, in so doing becoming the
first colony to break away without the mother country's

approval since the American Revolution. During the next years, regarding the departure as invalid, the London government banned all British trade with Rhodesia. The Security Council of the United Nations in 1966 added compulsory economic sanctions of its own, including a prohibition on the sale of oil to the country. Since that time, a number of Anglo-Rhodesian talks have attempted to restore amicable relations between the two countries, but all have failed. In 1969, Rhodesian voters approved the establishment of a republican form of government for the country and, at the same time, displaying a remarkable lack of logic, adopted a constitution whose provisions deprived the black African majority from ever acquiring a political voice of consequence.

The only other East African loss was chalked up in sparsely populated Somaliland. On July 1, 1960, at the close of a ten-year period of preparation by their colonial overlords, British Somaliland and Italian Somaliland joined forces to become a republic. The new country did not seek membership in the Commonwealth.

The rest of East Africa's story has been one of gain for the Commonwealth. Tanganyika, which had been a League of Nations mandate since World War I and a United Nations trust territory since World War II, administered throughout the years by Britain, was declared an independent nation on December 9, 1961. Two years and one day later, the tiny off-shore island of Zanzibar, a British protectorate since 1890, followed suit. Then within months— on April 24, 1964—the two united themselves into a single nation, the United Republic of Tanganyika and Zanzibar. Combining elements from each of their names, they rechristened the republic Tanzania in October of that year.

Kenya, which began its life under British rule as a colony and a protectorate, wrote an ugly page into its history in the early 1950s when Kikiyu natives rose against the whites occupying their plateau homeland and spread terror throughout the region with their Mau Mau movement. In 1954, responding to the rising nationalism that had triggered the movement and its savage killings, Britain began preparing the territory for independence, which came on July 12, 1963, with Kenya's transformation into a republic. Kenya's history since that date has been equally turbulent, with the country's intense nationalism causing it in the late 1960s to attempt to break the dominant grip that some 188,000 Indian inhabitants held on its trade. Instituted were repressive measures that caused some 20,000 of their number to flee the country.

Neighboring Uganda, a British protectorate since 1894, graduated to independence on October 9, 1962, becoming a republic. As in Kenya, much of its subsequent history has come of its intense nationalism. In 1970, Prime Minister Dr. Milton Obote pushed through laws requiring that the fifty thousand Asians who live in Uganda but retain British citizenship must hold a variety of passes and permits to continue residing and doing business there. Obote's new laws likewise called for all non-citizens of Uganda to be dismissed from employment.

Since then, Obote has been ousted, and in October 1972, as this is written, General Idi Amin Dada is in control of the nation. Amin ordered all Asiatics out of the country, giving them about three months to ready themselves for departure. In September 1972, some eight hundred Ugandan soldiers, who opposed Amin's rule, attempted an unsuccessful invasion of the country from camps they had established in neighboring Tanzania.

Despite their anti-European and anti-Asiatic policies, both Kenya and Uganda sought and were granted membership in the Commonwealth.

In northeast Africa, the Commonwealth story has been one of total loss, with Egypt escaping the British grasp nine years before the Statute of Westminster and the Sudan declaring itself independent in the mid-1950s and then remaining aloof from Commonwealth membership.

The British, after making Egypt a protectorate in 1914, encountered such a post-World War I wave of nationalism, marked by riots and uprisings, that they were driven to award the ancient country its independence in 1922. At the time, Britain retained the right to station troops in Egypt to protect her various interests there, chief among them the Suez Canal. In a 1936 agreement, all troops but those guarding the canal were removed. Then, in 1956, three years after revolutionary forces had ousted King Farouk and had declared the country a republic, President Gamal Abdel Nasser nationalized the canal zone and ordered all British representatives to head for home. Israel, barred from using the canal, invaded the Gaza Strip and the Sinai Peninsula, while Britain and France, seeing their own use of the canal jeopardized, launched an attack on Egypt. International pressures, however, brought the hostilities to a halt, with a U.N. emergency force then occupying the zone. All foreign troops pulled out of Egypt in 1957.

As for the Sudan: in 1924—after Egypt and Britain had held the Sudan as a condominium for a quarter century—

Egyptian troops there mutinied, their aim being to drive out Britain just as it had been driven from Egypt two years earlier. The British, however, crushed the mutiny and expelled all Egyptian officials, assuming complete control of the Sudan. Britain by itself governed the area until 1936 when a new agreement for its mutual Anglo-Egyptian supervision was reached.

With the end of World War II, however, the Sudanese began to press for independence, led by the most educated of their number. Together, Britain and Egypt, in 1953, undertook the job of readying the country for self-government by sponsoring an election in which an all-Sudanese parliament was to be installed in office and an all-Sudanese interim government was to be established. Under the arrangement, the Sudanese were then to spend three years determining the form of government their country would eventually take but, in 1955, an impatient Sudanese parliament suddenly declared the nation independent. Britain and Egypt agreed to the declaration, and the Sudan was proclaimed a republic on January 1, 1956. Since then, its history has been regularly marked with civil strife, with the Moslems of its northern regions pitted against the black Africans living in the south.

Though the northeast brought only losses, the moves to independence in the west netted only gains for the Commonwealth. There, Gambia, Sierra Leone, Ghana, and Nigeria all entered the Commonwealth upon separation from the mother country. Of the four Gambia and Ghana took the step to self-government most easily and most peacefully. For Sierra Leone and Nigeria, independence was accompanied by civil strife.

Gambia, a colony since 1843, and long a friend of the British because of their nineteenth-century anti-slavery efforts and their arbitration of early tribal disputes, won independence in February 1965, becoming both Africa's and the Commonwealth's smallest nation. In April 1970, an election determined that the country would function as a republic.

By the time Gambia departed the mother country in 1965, Ghana—whose coastal area had been made a colony in 1874 and its interior a protectorate in 1901—had been an independent nation for eight years, having acquired that status on March 6, 1957. A year earlier, the British sector of mandated Togoland was added to its territory as the result of a referendum. Ghana became a republic and a member of the Commonwealth on July 1, 1960.

Nigeria's independence came on October 1 of the same year, when it was organized as a loose federation of independent states that housed more than two hundred and fifty linguistic and ethnic groups. The British portion of the mandated Cameroon joined the federation in 1961, and two years later Nigeria adopted a republican form of government for itself. Since then, because of its many tribal elements and their ancient rivalries and hatreds, it has suffered much political unrest, which climaxed in a tragic upheaval in 1967 when Ibo tribesmen, fleeing the slaughters of their Hausa enemies, migrated from the country's north to its eastern regions. Once there, and again enduring the attacks of the Hausa, they were told that they must return to the north. They responded by seceding from the federation and declaring the eastern area to be the Republic of Biafra. The action led to a civil war of thirty-one months, in which thousands died in the fighting and the starvation that accompanied it. Biafra surrendered and returned to the federal system in January 1970.

Sierra Leone achieved independence as a parliamentary state within the Commonwealth in 1961 and voted itself a republic in 1971. In the intervening decade, however, this country—whose coast had been a colony since 1808 and whose inland regions had been protectorates since 1898—was torn with civil strife. The strife, centered about its two principal political factions—the Peoples Party and the All Peoples Congress Party—reached such proportions in the late 1960s over a constitutional crisis that the then governor-general, J. L. Boston, was forced to dissolve the Sierra Leone parliament and take the reins of government in his own hands for a time. Later in the year, the nation's military seized the government, only to fall to a 1968 coup by the All Peoples Congress Party which restored Sierra Leone to civilian authority.

More than forty years have elapsed since the Statute of Westminster was enacted in 1931 and made possible the transformation of Empire to Commonwealth. In that time, the Commonwealth, sustaining some losses along the way, has grown from its original seven members to a family of thirty-two nations. Of that number, we have thus far talked of twenty-four. The family is rounded out by Barbados, Guyana (formerly British Guiana), Jamaica, Nauru, Trinidad-Tobago, Fiji, Tonga, and Western Samoa, and by the dependencies of the United Kingdom, Australia and New Zealand, to be discussed in the next chapter.

Chapter Twelve

Commonwealth

If one word had to be chosen to describe the Commonwealth, that word should be "flexibility." It is that quality which, ever since India's request in 1949 to remain within the Commonwealth when she became an independent republic, has made possible the growth of the family of nations, remarkable now in the ethnic and governmental diversity of its members. Without it, the Commonwealth, because of the subsequent loss of South Africa and Eire and Newfoundland's marriage to Canada, might now be restricted to four members.

How did the Indian request reveal that flexibility?

When the Statute of Westminster was enacted, each of the overseas members swore allegiance to the British Crown and, in so doing, declared their governments to be monarchies, each independent of the other, but all under the reign of a single ruler. Aside from a frown by the Irish Free

253

State, there was no problem in securing the oath of allegiance, and even the Free State was willing to bow to it for the economic benefits of Commonwealth membership. All shared a common British background, a common language, as well as a traditional and, in most cases, sentimental loyalty to the Crown, including great segments of the Irish population.

But, with the Indian request, there came a problem. India, as Nehru put it, wanted to remain within the Commonwealth "because we think it is beneficial to us and to certain causes in the world that we wish to advance," adding that "In the world today, where there are so many disruptive forces at work, where we are often on the verge of war, I think it is not a safe thing to encourage the break-up of any association that one has . . . it is better to keep a cooperative association going which may do good in this world rather than break it." [25] And, as he knew, the Commonwealth wanted India to remain within its framework; she had much to offer in manpower, in resources, and in solid intellect. But she did not want to swear allegiance to the Crown. She did not want to become a monarchy under a British ruler. She had struggled too long for freedom to accept, in the end, such an arrangement. She solved the dilemma by declaring that, while she could not bring herself to allegiance, she could freely recognize the Crown as the symbol of Commonwealth and, consequently, as its head.

It was a fine point of differentiation, possibly one best suited to Indian logic, certainly a subtle political compromise, and most certainly one demanding a flexibility of attitude on the part of the Commonwealth prime ministers who met at London in 1949 to consider it.

And a flexibility of attitude was what it earned. The ministers agreed that it did not meet the precise requirements of the Statute of Westminster but that it was assuredly compatible with them. It was as fine a point as India had drawn. At the close of the meeting, the ministers issued a declaration that, in part, read:

"The Government of India have informed the other Governments of the Commonwealth of the intention of the Indian people that under a new constitution which is about to be adopted India shall become a sovereign independent republic. The Government of India have, however, declared and affirmed India's desire to continue her full membership in the Commonwealth of Nations and her acceptance of the King as the symbol of the free association of its independent nations, and as such the Head of the Commonwealth.

"The Governments of the other countries of the Commonwealth, the basis of whose membership of the Commonwealth is not hereby changed, accept and recognize India's continuing membership in accordance with the terms of this declaration." [26]

Thus, the Commonwealth welcomed its first republic and opened the way for admission to many non-British countries that, though desiring Commonwealth membership, might not in conscience, considering their histories as Empire holdings, have been able to swear allegiance to the Crown. If ever the British had been accused of insular snobbery, that charge could not be leveled here. With the ministers' declaration, the word British fell out of use in the family's title, which became, simply, the Commonwealth of Nations.

Thanks to this flexibility, the Commonwealth has been able to welcome to its ranks a variety of governments: monarchies, republics, federations, kingdoms, parliamentary democracies, and newly independent nations which have not yet determined their final governmental structure. It has even made room for a tiny Pacific island: Nauru. Located some two thousand miles northeast of Australia and with a population of just six thousand, Nauru is one of the world's chief sources of phosphate, producing approximately 1.6 million tons a year. A one-time German holding and a British-Australian-New Zealand mandate after World War I, Nauru has held a special membership in the Commonwealth since becoming a republic in 1968. It is not represented at Commonwealth meetings, but it is permitted to participate in other Commonwealth activities.

The varied states of the Commonwealth are listed below in alphabetical order, along with their governmental structures and their dates of entry into the family of nations.

State	Government	Date
1. Australia	Monarchy	1931
2. Barbados	Parliamentary Democracy	1966
3. Botswana	Republic	1965
4. Canada	Monarchy	1931
5. Ceylon	Monarchy	1948
6. Cyprus	Republic	1960
7. Fiji	Independent nation under a governor general	1970

State	Government	Date
8. Gambia	Republic	1965
9. Ghana	Republic	1960
10. Guyana	Republic	1966
11. India	Republic	1950
12. Jamaica	Monarchy	1962
13. Kenya	Republic	1963
14. Lesotho	Monarchy	1966
15. Malawi	Republic	1964
16. Malaysia	Federation	1963
17. Malta	Monarchy	1964
18. Mauritius	Monarchy	1968
19. Nauru	Republic	1968
20. New Zealand	Monarchy	1931
21. Nigeria	Republic	1960
22. Pakistan	Republic	1955
23. Sierra Leone	Republic	1961
24. Singapore	Republic	1965
25. Swaziland	Monarchy	1968
26. Tanzania	Republic	1964
27. Tonga	Kingdom	1970
28. Trinidad-Tobago	Monarchy	1962
29. Uganda	Republic	1962
30. United Kingdom	Monarchy	1931
31. Western Samoa	Monarchy	1962
32. Zambia	Republic	1964

Within the Commonwealth framework, Britain continues to hold her possessions from Empire days. Consisting of colonies, protectorates, crown dependencies, and condominiums, they range all across the world:

Holding	*Status*
Bahamas	Colony
Bermuda	Colony
British Antarctic Territory	Colony
British Honduras	Colony: At the time this is written, British Honduras, with a strong anti-British faction within its borders, is preparing for independence as the nation of Belize.
British Indian Ocean Territory	Colony: Consisting of the small Aldabra Islands, Farquhar Islands, Desroches Islands, and the Chagos Archipelago, this colony was established in 1965 under an agreement with the Mauritius and Seychelles islands.
British Virgin Islands	Colony
Canton and Enderbury Islands	Condominium: Located approximately 1,600 miles southeast of Hawaii, these islands are administered jointly by Britain and the United States under an agreement made in 1939.
Cayman Islands	Colony
Central and Southern Line Islands	Colony: These several islands, together occupying no more than thirty-six square miles and chiefly uninhabited, are located

Holding	*Status*
Central and Southern Line Islands	in the South Pacific, in the vicinity of the Gilbert and Ellice Islands.
Channel Islands	Crown Dependency
Falkland Islands	Colony
Gibraltar	Colony
Gilbert and Ellice Islands	Colony
Hong Kong	Colony
Isle of Man	Crown Dependency
Montserrat	Colony
New Hebrides Islands	Condominium: Numbering approximately forty and lying northeast of New Caledonia, these islands are administered jointly by Britain and France under an agreement made in 1906.
Pitcairn Island Group	Colony: The group consists of Pitcairn Island and three nearby uninhabited islands—Henderson, Ducie, and Oeno.
Rhodesia	Self-governing colony: Though Rhodesia has declared itself an independent country, Britain has not yet recognized the declaration.
St. Helena Island	Colony: A 47-square-mile island, St. Helena holds two dependencies—Ascension Island

Holding	*Status*
	some 700 miles to the northwest, and the Tristan da Cunha group, a cluster of six small islands approximately 1,500 miles to the southwest.
Seychelles Islands	Colony
Solomon Islands	Protectorate
Turks and Caicos Islands	Colony

Australia and New Zealand likewise hold dependencies within the Commonwealth, having been assigned them, in great part, because of their locations. With the exception of one, all are listed as territories.

The Australian dependencies are: Australian Antarctica; Christmas Island; Cocos Islands; Heard and McDonald islands; New Guinea (a U.N. trust territory); Norfolk Island; and Papua. The last is located on New Guinea and is administered jointly with the New Guinea trust territory.

The New Zealand dependencies are: The Cook Islands; Niue Island; the Ross Dependency in Antarctica; and the Tokelau Islands.

India also holds a dependency, the protectorate of Sikkim. Located in the northeast of India and wedged between Nepal on the west and Bhutan on the east, it became a British protectorate in 1890 via an agreement with China. On India's independence, it passed to the new republic.

Holding a special status within the Commonwealth are the islands making up the West Indies Associated States, an organization which was formed in 1967. Consisting of Antigua,

St. Kitts-Nevis-Anguilla, Dominica, Grenada, St. Lucia, and St. Vincent, the island-states stretch down through the Leeward and Windward chains between the Atlantic and the Caribbean. Under the terms of the association, they are listed as island territories, each of which is self-governing, and each of which holds the option for complete independence. The association between each state and Britain is maintained on a voluntary basis and may be terminated by either party. Such termination by Britain would, of course, result in the states becoming independent of the mother country. Housed within the Associated States is a federation made up of the three small islands of St. Kitts, Nevis, and Anguilla.

As did the Empire before it, the Commonwealth today occupies approximately one-quarter of the earth's land areas and houses about one-quarter of its peoples, entering all oceans and finding its way to every continent. And, as was said of Empire, it represents the most powerful and wealthiest amalgamation of states ever assembled in history.

It is, though, an arrangement far different from that of Empire. There are not within it the Navigation Acts of old; trade is carried on between the Commonwealth nations, and with other countries, for the benefit of the individual members and not for that of the mother country alone. Nor is there in it the arrogance that marked so much of the early Empire, when Elizabeth I stole Irish land and George III so infuriated the American colonies that they rose up in arms and brought the first Empire crashing down about London's ears. Nor the exploitation of a British East India Company with its freedom to disrupt an entire native economy so that it could pay its shareholders a satisfactory dividend. Nor (though the problem persists at a personal level in many quarters, for men, it seems, will always be men) the prejudices that relegated Indians to menial tasks only, that enabled the first white Tasmanians to hunt down natives for the sport of it, and that allowed the infection of apartheid to spread in Rhodesia and among the British segments in South Africa; were the prejudices now sanctioned at Commonwealth level, the present-day status of Rhodesia and South Africa assuredly would not be what it is.

The Commonwealth maintains the best of the British spirit as it was seen in the Empire. There is, first, the same intelligent outlook that enabled British statesmen to turn their cherished Empire into the Commonwealth in the first place. It made them see clearly that the attitudes of people across the world were changing and that the changes would make impossible the continuance of something so authoritarian as an Empire. Rather than fight the changing attitudes—a fight that would have caused the Empire to die in chaos, for the old has rarely been able to withstand the onslaught of the new—they had sense enough to save their holdings by forming them into a family of equal nations. Just as it gave birth to the Commonwealth, so has this intelligence kept the family intact through the years despite periodic differences among the various member states.

There is, second, the traditional loyalty to the Crown. It prompted many holdings to contribute men to the British cause in World War I when the Empire was approaching its zenith, and again in World War II, long after the Empire ceased to be. Not to have gone to the aid of the United Kingdom would have been, in the eyes of countless men who had never seen her, unthinkable. This same loyalty today causes many Commonwealth members to go on acknowledging the Crown as the head of the family of nations when they are far larger, far stronger, and far wealthier than the former mother country.

Finally, there is in Britain herself that liberal spirit of old, best exemplified in men such as Lord Durham, William Gladstone, and Arthur Balfour, which prompted her to award many of her holdings an increasing degree of self-government throughout the course of Empire. Then in the days of Commonwealth, it enabled her to assist many of her possessions in attaining full independence. It also made it possible for her to offer the holdings the free choice of joining or not joining the Commonwealth. Today, it is responsible for her policy of helping to develop the political and economic responsibilities of her remaining holdings so that they may be fully ready for the impending day of independence.

In 1931 and the years following, the sun of Empire went down on the British lion. In the Commonwealth, he found a new day.

Notes

(1) Heading the list of Empire exports were thirty-five products. Graphically illustrating the Empire's varied riches, they were: asbestos, bananas, cocoa, coffee, copper, cotton, dairy produce, diamonds, gum arabic, hides, iron, jute, kerosene, machinery, manganese, meat, medicinal drugs, newsprint, oil seed, palm kernels, palm oil, petroleum, rubber, rum, sisal, steel, sugar, tea, tin, tobacco, vehicles, wheat, wood, wool, and zinc.

(2) Quoted in Leacock, Stephen, *The British Empire,* page 9; Dodd Mead, New York, 1940

(3) Quoted in Eckles, Robert B. and Hale, Richard W., *Britain, Her Peoples and the Commonwealth,* page 113; McGraw-Hill, New York, 1954

(4) Discussed in Bailey, Thomas A., *The American Pageant—A History of the Republic,* pages 11–12; D. C. Heath, Boston, 1956

(5) Discussed in Burke, Merle, *United States History—The Growth of Our Land,* page 20; American Technical Society, Chicago, 1957

(6) Creighton, Donald, *The Story of Canada,* page 129; Houghton Mifflin, Boston, 1960

(7) Discussed in Brown, Joe David, and the Editors of *Life, India,* page 63; Time Incorporated, New York, 1961

(8) Quoted in Eckles and Hale, *Britain, Her Peoples and the Commonwealth,* page 355, *op. cit.*

(9) Discussed in Graham, Gerald S., *A Concise History of the British Empire,* pages 42–43; Viking Press, New York, 1971

(10) *India,* page 65

(11) Quoted in *India,* page 64

(12) *A Concise History of the British Empire,* page 45

(13) Discussed in Hall, Walter Phelps and Albion, Robert Greenhalgh, with the collaboration of Jennie Barnes Pope, *A History of England and the British Empire,* pages 673–674; Ginn and Company, Boston, 1946

(14) *Ibid.,* page 674

(15) Figure given is according to 1966 census; it includes Madagascar, the Canary Islands, the Comoro Islands, and other off-shore islands.

(16) *A Concise History of the British Empire,* page 186

(17) The precise dates of the first departures have long been a source of historical dispute, with some authorities dating the start of the movement as early as 1831 and as late as 1836. It is known, however, that scouting parties were checking the northern terrain in 1834 and that some wagons were on the move in 1835.

(18) Hopkinson, Tom, and the Editors of *Life, South Africa,* page 63; Time Incorporated, New York, 1964

(19) MacManus, Seumas, *The Story of the Irish Race,* pages 403–404; Devin-Adair, New York, 1944 (fourth revised edition)

(20) *Ibid.,* page 485

(21) *Encyclopedia Britannica,* vol. 4, page 178; Encyclopedia Britannica, Incorporated, Chicago, 1957

(22) *India,* page 66

(23) *A Concise History of the British Empire,* page 253

(24) From an August 20, 1917, speech in the House of Commons by E. S. Montagu, the Secretary of State for India, *Encyclopedia Britannica,* vol. 12, page 173

(25) *Encyclopedia Britannica,* vol. 4, page 186

(26) *Ibid.,* page 185

Bibliography

Bailey, Thomas A.: *The American Pageant—A History of the Republic,* D. C. Heath, Boston, 1956

Brown, Joe David, and the Editors of *Life*: *India,* Time Inc., New York, 1961

Burke, Merle: *United States History—The Growth of Our Land,* American Technical Society, Chicago, 1957

Careless, J. M. S., and Brown, R. Craig: *The Canadians, 1867–1967,* Macmillan of Canada, Toronto, 1967

Carty, James, editor: *Ireland—From the Great Famine to the Treaty of 1921,* C. J. Fallon, Dublin, 1966 (4th edition)

Coughlan, Robert, and the Editors of *Life*: *Tropical Africa,* Time Inc., New York, 1966

Creighton, Donald: *The Story of Canada,* Houghton Mifflin, Boston, 1960

Cross, Colin: *The Fall of the British Empire, 1918–1968,* Coward McCann, New York, 1968

Daggs, Elisa: *All Africa,* Hastings House, New York, 1970

Debenham, Frank: *Discovery and Exploration,* Crescent Books, London, 1960

Eckles, Robert B., and Hale, Richard W.: *Britain, Her Peoples and the Commonwealth,* McGraw-Hill, New York, 1954

Gardner, Brian: *The African Dream,* Putnam, New York, 1970

Graham, Gerald S.: *A Concise History of the British Empire,* Viking, New York, 1971

Hall, Walter Phelps, and Albion, Robert Greenhalgh, with the collaboration of Jennie Barnes Pope: *A History of England and the British Empire,* Ginn, Boston, 1946

Hopkinson, Tom, and the Editors of *Life*: *South Africa,* Time Inc., New York, 1964

Leacock, Stephen: *The British Empire—Its Structure, Its Unity, Its Strength,* Dodd Mead, New York, 1940

MacManus, Seumas: *The Story of the Irish Race,* Devin-Adair, New York, 1944 (4th revised edition)

Mansergh, Nicholas: *The Commonwealth Experience,* Praeger, New York, 1969

McClellan, Grant S., editor: *India,* H. W. Wilson, New York, 1960

Moore, Clark D., and Dunbar, Ann, editors: *Africa Yesterday and Today,* Bantam, New York, 1968

Moore, Brian, and the Editors of *Life*: *Canada,* Time Inc., New York, 1963

Oliver, Roland, and Fage, J. D.: *A Short History of Africa,* Penguin Books, Baltimore, 1962

Ross, Frances Aileen: *The Land and People of Canada,* Lippincott, New York, 1964

Ryan, A. P.: *Islands Apart—The Story of Ireland from St. Patrick to De Valera,* Morrow, New York, 1954

Shaw, A. G. L.: *A Short History of Australia,* Praeger, New York, 1967

Sinclair, Keith: *A History of New Zealand,* Penguin, Baltimore, 1959

Spear, Percival: *India—A Modern History,* University of Michigan Press, Ann Arbor, 1961

Tennant, Kylie: *Australia—Her Story,* St. Martin's, New York, 1933

Thompson, William Irwin: *The Imagination of an Insurrection— Dublin, Easter 1916,* Oxford University Press, New York, 1967

Trupin, James E.: *West Africa,* Parents' Magazine Press, New York, 1971

Wall, Daphne: *The Story of the Commonwealth,* Watts, New York, 1960

Walton, Richard J.: *Canada and the U.S.A.,* Parents' Magazine Press, New York, 1972

Williams, Desmond, editor: *The Irish Struggle, 1916–1926,* Routledge and Kegan Paul, London, 1966

Yeats-Brown, F.: *The Pageant of India,* Macrae-Smith, Philadelphia, 1942

Index